MW01596220

S[eek God]
for the
CITY 2020

It's hard to pray beyond our own problems, especially in difficult times. But since our God does great things in the midst of troubled times, now is actually the best time to pray beyond ourselves with expansive prayers of solid hope. We will either find God-given courage to pray great things, or we will find that our hope, along with our love, will grow cold.

Reviving hope. This edition of *Seek God for the City* is designed to re-ignite desires for Christ that may have gone dormant, so that our hope in Christ and His kingdom will rise again.

Seeking His face. Seeking His kingdom.
We will seek God in two simple ways: First, we'll seek God's face, and then we'll seek God's kingdom. As we come to Him – seeking His face, He will come to us – bringing His kingdom.

Consider these prayers to be an incendiary device, rekindling your faith and love in heart-blazing hope of what our King Jesus desires.

Yours in hope for Christ's glory,

Steve Hawthorne

Steve Hawthorne for WayMakers

Praying in full-hearted hope

A different way each day to pray in biblical hope

Pray the heart of God with selected verses from the Old Testament, and then another passage from the Gospels on the same theme. Since the prayers express God's ancient purposes in contemporary ways, you can pray with courage and clarity.

Daily: the different people of your community.

Each day prompts you to stretch your prayers for specific people who are part of any community, such as orphans, business people, police, pastors, gangs, elderly people, homeless people, and many more. By praying for each one, you will pray for everyone in your city more than once.

Countries of the world

Each day lists a few countries of the world. Why not name at least one or two countries every day?

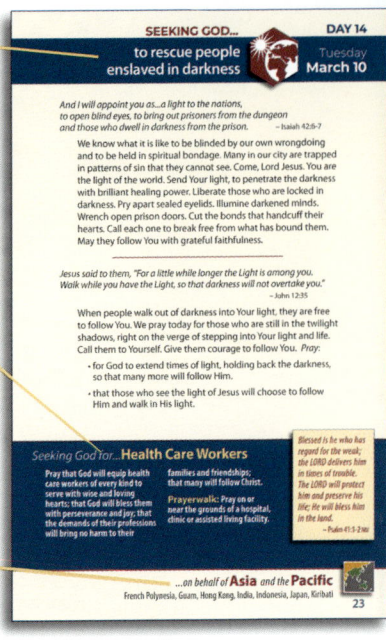

SEEKING GOD...
to rescue people enslaved in darkness

DAY 14
Tuesday
March 10

And I will appoint you as...a light to the nations,
to open blind eyes, to bring out prisoners from the dungeon
and those who dwell in darkness from the prison.   – Isaiah 42:6-7

We know what it is like to be blinded by our own wrongdoing and to be held in spiritual bondage. Many in our city are trapped in patterns of sin that they cannot see. Come, Lord Jesus. You are the light of the world. Send Your light, to penetrate the darkness with brilliant healing power. Liberate those who are locked in darkness. Pry apart sealed eyelids. Illumine darkened minds. Wrench open prison doors. Cut the bonds that handcuff their hearts. Call each one to break free from what has bound them. May they follow You with grateful faithfulness.

Jesus said to them, "For a little while longer the Light is among you. Walk while you have the Light, so that darkness will not overtake you."   – John 12:35

When people walk out of darkness into Your light, they are free to follow You. We pray today for those who are still in the twilight shadows, right on the verge of stepping into Your light and life. Call them to Yourself. Give them courage to follow You. Pray:

• for God to extend times of light, holding back the darkness, so that many more will follow Him.

• that those who see the light of Jesus will choose to follow Him and walk in His light.

Blessed is he who has regard for the weak; the LORD delivers him in times of trouble. The LORD will protect him and preserve his life; He will bless him in the land.
– Psalm 41:1-2 NIV

Seeking God for...**Health Care Workers**

Pray that God will equip health care workers of every kind to serve with wise and loving hearts; that God will bless them with perseverance and joy; that the demands of their professions will bring no harm to their

families and friendships; that many will follow Christ.

Prayerwalk: Pray on or near the grounds of a hospital, clinic or assisted living facility.

...on behalf of **Asia** and the **Pacific**
French Polynesia, Guam, Hong Kong, India, Indonesia, Japan, Kiribati

23

Prayers can open the Scriptures.

Scripture deepens your praying

A good way to pray these prayers:

It's as simple as reading the verses before *and after* reading the prayer.

1. Read the Bible verses. Out loud is best. It usually takes only 10-20 seconds.

2. Pray the written prayer. As you read, give God access to your imagination, looking through the lens of His word on your community.

3. Then read the Bible verses again. After going through the prayer, most people find it helpful to re-read the Bible verses. As you do, you'll see how the prayer springs directly from the Bible, deepening and strengthening your praying.

Get the app.
Pray anytime, anywhere.

Get *Seek God 2020* as an app on your tablet or smartphone. The app contains all of the same scriptures, prayers and helpful material. The app makes it easier to pray anytime or anywhere. Available December 2019. Check out a preview at **waymakers.org**. Tell your friends in other cities and countries about the app.

iOS   Android

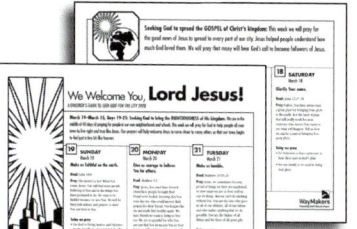

Help the kids pray with you.
Use the children's version.

A free, downloadable kid's version is available in "pdf" format on our website. It's a great resource to engage kids in this prayer adventure! Find it at **waymakers.org**.

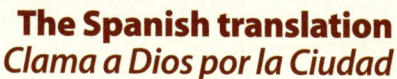

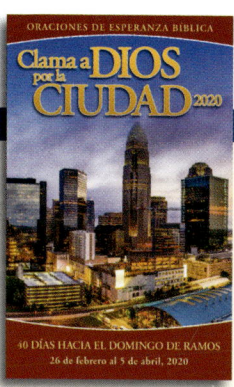

The Spanish translation
Clama a Dios por la Ciudad

Invite Spanish-speaking friends to pray with *Seek God* in Spanish. It's called *Clama a Dios por la Ciudad 2020*. The 64-page booklet is available at the same low cost as the English version. Available December 2019.

Find and share practical ideas.

Use the helpful resources at **waymakers.org**. Find practical ways to remind your church family to pray, such as bulletin inserts and powerpoint slides.

Share what you are praying.

Interact with others about what you like about the prayers at **Facebook.com/seekgodforthecity**.

Seeking His FACE
Opening up to know God

*Return to Me,
...that I may
return to you.*

– Zechariah 1:3

Two parts to this 40-day season

During the first 11 days we will seek God's *face*.
The rest of the time, we will seek God's *kingdom*.

Everyone seeks Him.

Seeking God's face is not something just for ministers
and mystics. God has shaped and called every human
alive to know Him personally – to seek His face.

The joy of being known by God

We are invited to seek God in face-to-face nearness.
As you bring yourself to God you aren't trying, of course,
to physically see Him. Knowing God is really a matter of
being known by God (Galatians 4:9), allowing Him to gaze
upon your open life. As you turn your attention toward
Him, His love will examine you, lift you and change you.

Return to Me – and I will return to you.

To seek God's face means that we are coming to God.
To seek God's kingdom means that we are calling for
God to come to us. These things go together. We may
not be able to do either without doing both.

More than once God told His people, "Return to Me, and I
will return to you" (Malachi 3:7, also Zechariah 1:3). We are
seeking God's face, not because He is hiding; not because
He is hard to find. He has not left us. Instead, every person
has turned from God. We all find ways to keep ourselves
distant from Him.

As we come to Him, He comes to us.

Special times for turning

At special times God makes it possible for an entire people to reverse their course, and together make a U-turn back toward Him. Not all times are equal. Many sense that in these days, God is calling people all over the world to seek Him as never before.

Hearing God's call to seek His face

As we come to Him, we can have confidence to pray that He will come to us. David heard God's call to seek His face and made it a lifelong pursuit. In Psalm 27 David says,

> *One thing I ask of the LORD, this is what I seek:*
> *that I may dwell in the house of the LORD*
> *all the days of my life,*
> *to gaze upon the beauty of the LORD*
> *and to seek Him in His temple (Psalm 27:4 NIV).*

Solid hope: The goodness of God in the land of the living

Later in the same Psalm, David says,

> *I am still confident of this:*
> *I will see the goodness of the LORD*
> *in the land of the living (Psalm 27:13 NIV).*

As David sought God's face, he grew in confident hope that God would bring His transforming goodness into the predicaments in which David and his people lived. That is why he called for a persistent kind of prayer that would not let go of God's promised goodness:

> *Wait for the LORD; be strong and take heart*
> *and wait for the LORD (Psalm 27:14 NIV).*

David sought God's face, which led him to seek God's kingdom in full-hearted hope.

Not all times are equal. Sometimes God makes it possible for an entire people to make a U-turn back toward Him.

Seeking God's FACE

WEEK 1 FEBRUARY 26 - MARCH 7

This "week" (actually 11 days, beginning on Ash Wednesday, February 26) we will focus our prayers on seeking God's face.

We will pray with Psalm 24, in which the psalmist asks, "Who can ascend to the hill of the Lord?" When we hear this question, we too easily disqualify ourselves from approaching God. Instead, we can allow this question to be an invitation to us. By His death and risen life, Christ has made it possible for us to approach God and to be changed by Him. He desires for us to know Him better by drawing nearer.

Open your life to God. He summons you to seek His face. Accept His invitation to draw near.

This is the generation of those who seek Him, who seek Your face.
– Psalm 24:6

During the 40 days, we will pray for the continental areas of the earth in reverse sequence of Acts 1:8. We begin at the areas of the earth that are farthest from Jerusalem. We'll start by praying for the continents of South and North America and the Caribbean.

Seeking God on behalf of the **Americas** *and the* **Caribbean**

When You said, "Seek My face," my heart said to You,
"Your face, O LORD, I shall seek." – Psalm 27:8

We have heard Your voice calling to us. Yet too often we have allowed the noise of life to obscure Your call. Although we've ignored You before, we now hush our hearts long enough to respond to Your voice. You are calling, "Come! Come nearer! Come seek My face!" Our hearts answer back to You, "Yes! I'm coming! I will seek Your face!" This really is the deepest longing of our hearts. This is what we were made for: To know You. To come near You. To love You. We seek You because You first sought us. Please keep calling us, and we will keep coming.

Jesus...led them up on a high mountain...A bright cloud overshadowed them, and behold, a voice out of the cloud said, "This is My beloved Son, with whom I am well-pleased. Listen to Him!" – Matthew 17:1, 5

Lord Jesus, only You can bring us closer to God. We have wondered if nearness to God is something attained only by spiritual mystics. But if You bring us, we can come near, just as we are. As we stand with You, listening, we can sense the Father's love for You. His pleasure with You is because of His vast love for You. Persuade our hearts that the Father desires to enfold us in that same amazing love. Train us to listen to Your voice, Lord Jesus, to walk in the Father's great love. *Pray:*

• for God's people to hear His call to seek His face.

• for the Father to reveal His great love for people.

Seeking God for...**Youth**

Pray for teens to commit their lives to Christ; for older mentors; for authentic friendships with their peers who are following Jesus; for open trust and communication with parents; for God's intentions for their generation to come forth in fullest measure.

Prayerwalk: Pray with your eyes open for people in their teens. Envision them following Christ five, ten or more years from now.

Let our sons in their youth be as grown-up plants, and our daughters as corner pillars fashioned as for a palace...How blessed are the people whose God is the LORD!
– Psalm 144:12, 15

...on behalf of the **Americas** *and the* **Caribbean**
Anguilla, Antigua and Barbuda, Argentina, Aruba, Bahamas

for assurance of His forgiveness

Who may ascend into the hill of the LORD?
And who may stand in His holy place?
He who has clean hands *and a pure heart...*   – Psalm 24:3-4

Father God, Your Son did not die merely to free us from the guilt of our sins. Your Son died to bring us near to You. Memories of our sins still haunt us, convincing us that our hearts remain stained with shame. Despite Your marvelous forgiveness, we continue to shy away from Your presence. But no longer. We set aside foolish thoughts that we are not wanted or tolerated in Your presence. By the cleansing power of Jesus' death, we lift clean hands to You. We gladly approach You now in grateful praise.

When the disciples heard this, they fell face down to the ground and were terrified. And Jesus came to them and touched them and said, "Get up, and do not be afraid."   – Matthew 17:6-7

We have accepted Your pardon, yet sometimes we find ourselves paralyzed in fear. Touch us just as You touched Your frightened friends so long ago. As before, command us to rise and to follow You without fear. *Pray:*

- for Jesus to give many people the boldness to faithfully follow Him.

- for Christ to touch those who are paralyzed in guilt so that they will joyfully serve God.

I know that the LORD will maintain the cause of the afflicted and justice for the poor.
   – Psalm 140:12

Seeking God for...**the Poor**

Pray that the spiritual and physical needs of the poor will be met with dignity and stability. Pray that God will release them from cycles of oppression and despair so that the poor are transformed to become God's blessing for others.

Prayerwalk: Walk in places of poverty and neglect. Ask the Holy Spirit to give you His eyes and His heart in order to pray in hope, not from pity. What grieves or gladdens God as He walks amidst the poor?

...on behalf of the **Americas** *and the* **Caribbean**

Barbados, Belize, Bermuda, Bolivia, Brazil

to give us pure hearts

Who may ascend into the hill of the LORD?
And who may stand in His holy place?
He who has clean hands **and a pure heart...**   – Psalm 24:3-4

We have been summoned to come before You, into Your courts of splendor, as if we hold in our hands engraved invitations. We pause to check the date again. You want us to come now, before eternity, while we are living on the earth, so that we might begin to taste the love of heaven. The forgiveness of Jesus should remove any hesitation. Our sinful past no longer marks us. We cannot trust our wayward hearts, but we refuse to doubt Your heart and Your word. You are for us! You have promised to change us, inside and throughout. Surely Your favor will prevail! In hope that You will make our hearts pure, we boldly come to You.

And lifting up their eyes, they saw no one except Jesus Himself alone. – Matthew 17:8

We are easily distracted by minor things. Capture the full attention of our hearts. Turn our eyes to You. Exalt Jesus in our view so that lesser loves are eclipsed by His beauty and glory. *Pray:*

- for Jesus to be recognized as the singular Son of God, not merely one of many religious teachers.

- for the unique beauty of Jesus to be revealed, capturing the affection and devotion of many.

...but everyone who is fully trained will be like their teacher.
– Luke 6:40 NIV

Seeking God for...**Educators**

Pray that teachers and mentors will impart godly wisdom to help form character in their students; for needed tools and proper facilities; for those who home-school their children; for renewed zeal for truth and virtue; that they would have opportunity to know God in Christ; that believers would know how to pray for their students.

Prayerwalk: As you walk around or near a school, pray for teachers, administrators and other staff.

...on behalf of the **Americas** *and the* **Caribbean**
British Virgin Islands, Canada, Cayman Islands, Chile, Colombia

Saturday
February 29

to forsake falsehood

Who may ascend to the hill of the LORD?
And who may stand in His holy place?
He who has clean hands and a pure heart,
who has not lifted up his soul to falsehood and has not sworn deceitfully.
– Psalm 24:3-4

To gain the approval of others, we sometimes speak or act falsely. We know how to partition our lives to hide our white lies or our dalliance with idolatrous things. We may succeed in sustaining such a masquerade with people, but no disguise can fool You. Holy God, we approach You now with full disclosure. Today we confess any duplicity. We come to You clean and free in Christ. Liberate us from what entangles us. We renounce every false reliance and entrust ourselves entirely to You.

———————————————————

Jesus saw Nathanael coming to Him, and said of him,
"Behold, an Israelite indeed, in whom there is no deceit!"   – John 1:47

You saw Nathanael and saw his sincerity and desire for God. As we draw near to You, we know that Your gaze misses nothing. You know all about our mixed motives. Yet, in the midst of all that is phony or foolish, You also see the beginnings of a new integrity imparted by Your Spirit. Give us hope that You will continue to transform us to be true and clean in Your sight. *Pray:*

- that Your people will walk in God-given integrity.

- for those caught up in deception and hypocrisy to encounter Jesus so that the truth sets them free.

He saw a large crowd, and felt compassion for them and healed their sick.
– Matthew 14:14

Seeking God for...**Sick People**

Pray for God to touch those who are sick in your community with healing and comfort. Pray that they will grow in grace as God walks with them throughout their ordeal; that God will provide for their financial needs; for their caregivers and families; that many will renew their trust in Christ and follow Him boldly, even in affliction.

Prayerwalk: Consider those in your neighborhood who may be struggling with chronic illness or pain. Pray for their healing.

...on behalf of the **Americas** *and the* **Caribbean**
Costa Rica, Cuba, Dominica, Dominican Republic, Ecuador

for passion
to know and worship God

Sunday
March 1

He shall receive a blessing from the LORD
and righteousness from the God of his salvation.
This is the generation of those who seek Him,
who seek Your face – even as Jacob. — Psalm 24:5-6

Jacob was our father in faith, but he appeared to lack integrity. He was devious in some of his dealings. Yet he was ambitious to obtain Your blessing, willing to wrestle angels, refusing to let go in order to be blessed. We desire the audacity of Jacob – to seek Your face even as he did. We have come to You in the righteousness of Jesus. Add to us now the zeal of Jacob. One day there will be a generation that will seek for more than Your blessing. They will seek Your face and never let go. Let us be this promised generation, young and old together, who will seek Your face with lasting passion.

But an hour is coming, and now is, when the true worshipers
will worship the Father in spirit and truth; for such people
the Father seeks to be His worshipers. — John 4:23

An hour will come when You will receive what You have long sought: a people worshiping You in spirit and in truth. Keep seeking those who seek You in our city. Find and form a generation of true worshipers. *Pray:*

- for people to be filled with passion to love and serve God.

- that the Father would gather a generation of full-hearted worshipers in our city.

Seeking God for...Ethnic Communities

Pray that God will bring racial harmony; that long-standing offenses may be healed by the forgiveness that begins in Jesus; that Christians show honor and serve others in Christ's reconciling power; that the beauty of distinctive languages and cultures would be on display in local churches.

Prayerwalk: Pray blessings in a neighborhood with an ethnic identity different than your own, or pray blessings upon a business owned by people of another ethnicity than yours.

All the ends of the earth will remember and turn to the LORD, and all the families of the nations will bow down before Him.
— Psalm 22:27 NIV

...on behalf of the **Americas** *and the* **Caribbean**
El Salvador, Falkland Islands, French Guiana, Greenland

**Monday
March 2**

for freedom from conflicted desires

*O God, You are my God; I shall seek You earnestly.
        My soul thirsts for You, my flesh yearns for You,
        in a dry and weary land where there is no water.
Thus I have seen You in the sanctuary, to see Your power and Your glory.
Because Your lovingkindness is better than life, my lips will praise You.* – Psalm 63:1-3

Things of the world seem so desirable, almost drinkable, like a glimmering mirage in a desert. But such illusions disappoint us. We have tasted only sand. We still thirst with a deep-down loneliness. This thirst at the center of our soul is a yearning for You. And so we come to You to drink deeply. Nothing else will really satisfy. Being loved by You is far better than anything we might experience in life. We now make a choice: We will seek You. Early, often, and daily, we will seek Your face.

---

*But the Lord answered and said to her, "Martha, Martha,
you are worried and bothered about so many things,
but only one thing is necessary, for Mary has chosen the good part,
which shall not be taken away from her."* – Luke 10:41-42

Arrest our attention. Expose the shallow, useless things that absorb and distract us. Singularize our lives. Align our scattered desires into one holy passion to know You. *Pray:*

- for many to embrace the great value of knowing Christ above all other things.

- for Christ to simplify fragmented lives so that many will serve Him with undivided hearts.

*Blessed are they
who maintain justice,
who constantly do
what is right.*
– Psalm 106:3 NIV

Seeking God for... Law Enforcement *and* Judge

Pray for godly wisdom and Christ-like integrity; for physical and emotional protection; for courage and blessing for their families. Pray that they will become agents of God's hand to resist evil and bring an environment in which heaven's justice can increase.

Prayerwalk: Pray outside a police station, courthouse or a place of judicial administration. Consider leaving a short personal note for police, judges or court workers letting them know how Christians are praying for them today.

...on behalf of the **Americas** *and the* **Caribbean**
Grenada, Guadeloupe, Guatemala, Guyana, Haiti

for humility before God

If My people, who are called by My name,
will humble themselves and pray and seek My face
and turn from their wicked ways,
then will I hear from heaven
and will forgive their sin and will heal their land. – 2 Chronicles 7:14 NIV

Since we carry Your name as Your people, our sins have not only brought You sorrow, they have also brought shame to Your name. Even though some of us might live exemplary lives, many have disgraced Your reputation. Give us humility to recognize how we, as Your people, may have offended You in our generation. Only Your Spirit can give us genuine humility, not to berate ourselves, but to return to You. We confess: It is not all about us and our feelings of guilt. It is all about You, the grief of Your heart and the glory that You deserve. And so now we come, seeking Your face, and seeking Your glory.

Whoever then humbles himself as this child,
he is the greatest in the kingdom of heaven. – Matthew 18:4

Children usually see older people as bigger and greater than themselves. Give us the eyes of a child to see You as a great Father. Disclose to us how precious we are to You as Your adopted children. Give us childlike joy in exalting You and honoring others. *Pray:*

- that many would return home to the Father in genuine humility.
- for Christians to aspire to the greatness of serving Jesus.

Seeking God for... Mothers

Pray that God will refresh mothers in the honor and glory of motherhood; that they will be strengthened with grace, wisdom and love in serving their children; that they will be loved, protected and served by committed husbands; that mothers will model and express God's own nurturing love.

Prayerwalk: Walk through your neighborhood, praying for mothers and grandmothers.

She is clothed with strength and dignity; she can laugh at the days to come. She speaks with wisdom... Her children arise and call her blessed; her husband also, and he praises her.
– Proverbs 31:25-26, 28 NIV

...on behalf of the **Americas** *and the* **Caribbean**
Honduras, Jamaica, Martinique, Mexico, Montserrat

When you and your children return to the LORD your God...
He will circumcise your hearts and the hearts of your descendants,
so that you may love Him with all your heart
and with all your soul, and live. — Deuteronomy 30:2, 6 NIV

Bring the promised day when whole families will turn at the same time and come back to You together. We dare to imagine children, along with their parents, opening their lives to You. Call us to come to You with confidence and hope that we shall be changed – to love You more than ever before. You know that our hearts so easily wander, dividing our loyalties and fragmenting our lives. As we turn to You, reach into the interior of our lives as though You were performing open-heart surgery. Transform us from within. Give us love for You that grows steadily throughout our lives.

You have left your first love.
Therefore remember from where you have fallen,
and repent and do the deeds you did at first... — Revelation 2:4-5

We can recall how we loved You when our hearts were new in You. We have wandered from that love. Awaken us to love You as before.
Pray:

- for Christ to restore believers who have drifted from their first love.

- for those who have never loved or known Jesus to meet Him and to follow Him with obedient, joy-filled love.

Blessed are all who fear the LORD, who walk in His ways. You will eat the fruit of your labor; blessings and prosperity will be yours.
— Psalm 128:1-2 NIV

Seeking God for...**Laborers**

Pray that God will reveal the dignity and honor of doing work as unto Christ; that workplaces would be a setting of safety, joy and friendship; for workers to be treated with justice and dignity; for continued employment in the changing global economy; for many to follow Christ and serve Him openly in the workplace with co-laborers.

Prayerwalk: Find a way to walk and pray near a factory, construction site or another place of industry.

...on behalf of the **Americas** *and the* **Caribbean**
Netherlands Antilles, Nicaragua, Panama, Paraguay, Peru

to unite His people

So Judah gathered together to seek help from the LORD.
They even came from all the cities of Judah to seek the LORD...
"For we are powerless before this great multitude who are coming against us;
nor do we know what to do, but our eyes are on You." – 2 Chronicles 20:4, 12

Fear unites people when they are threatened by a common enemy.
Such momentary unity only lasts as long as the threat of terror.
We ask today for a greater unity among Your people that grows
by sharing a common love for You. Gather us to seek You in this
day of trouble. We are no different than Your people long ago:
We don't know what to do. We see no easy solutions. We simply
seek You, keeping our eyes fixed upon You. We remember Your great
deeds of the past. We savor Your promise for the difficult days ahead.
We wait, with eyes open, humbled and hopeful for Your glory.

I have other sheep, which are not of this fold;
I must bring them also, and they will hear My voice;
and they will become one flock with one shepherd. – John 10:16

Rival leaders have divided us. Common causes have failed to hold us.
Gather Your scattered, broken flock. Assemble us as one united people.
Lift Your voice over us. Make Your presence known and lead us like
a mighty shepherd. *Pray:*

- for Jesus to call His "other sheep," people who are now far from Him.

- for Christ to bring unity among churches, forming respect
  and relationships among leaders and people.

Seeking God for... Broken Families

Pray for the healing of broken
or bitter relationships. Ask God
to bring His comfort when family
members have passed away.
Pray that the Father heart of
God will overshadow children of
shattered families; that God will
meet financial needs, introduce
supportive friends and give them
hope in Christ.

Prayerwalk: Apartment
buildings often house
fragmented families. Pray
around an apartment complex,
focusing prayers on those who
have been bereaved or divorced.

The LORD...supports
the fatherless and
the widow.
 – Psalm 146:9

...on behalf of the **Americas** *and the* **Caribbean**

Puerto Rico, Saint Kitts and Nevis, Saint Lucia, Saint Pierre and Miquelon

Friday
March 6

for an outpouring of His Spirit

I will pour water on the thirsty ground and
send streams coursing through the parched earth.
I will pour My Spirit into your descendants and My blessing on your children.
They shall sprout like grass on the prairie, like willows alongside creeks.
This one will say, "I am God's," ...That one will write on his hand "God's property."
– Isaiah 44:3-5 The Message

You have promised that Your Spirit will descend like flooding streams, a force of life making parched places come alive. Cause this river to rush, bringing forth new sprouts of life in the withered places of our city. Young followers of Jesus will spring up, as numerous as grass blades and as powerful as trees. Infuse them with ferocious passion. Make these children to be Your champions. Give them exuberant loyalty, so they find joy in the very idea of belonging to You. Your name will be their identity and their jealousy. Their love for You will be on public display, as if they had etched Your name on their hands.

"If anyone is thirsty, let him come to Me and drink. He who believes in Me,
as the Scripture said, 'From his innermost being shall flow rivers of living water.'"
But this He spoke of the Spirit...
– John 7:37-39

Send Your Spirit like a river upon those who seek You. *Pray:*

- that God would surprise many who seek Him with a mighty outpouring of His Spirit.
- for believers to become open rivers of God's life to others.

One who is unmarried is concerned about the things of the Lord, how he may please the Lord.
– 1 Corinthians 7:32

Seeking God for...**Single People**

Pray that Christ will fill singles' hearts with His love; that they may taste the satisfaction found only in God; that friendships will bring ample fullness of relationship; for sexual purity and simplicity of lifestyle; and strong marriages for those who desire them. Pray for those who are single by divorce or death, that they would find healing and new hope for life ahead.

Prayerwalk: Pray for God's blessing upon people you see today who are single. Consider their story. Pray for their future and their hopes.

...on behalf of the **Americas** and the **Caribbean**

Saint Vincent and the Grenadines, Suriname, Trinidad and Tobago, Turks and Caicos Islands

to manifest His presence

How blessed are the people who know the joyful sound!
O LORD, they walk in the light of Your countenance.
In Your name they rejoice all the day. – Psalm 89:15-16

Grant to us this blessing: that together – as a people – we would hear the distant sound of Your oncoming majesty. It's like the peal of faraway trumpets. Amplify that sound so that it pierces our collective heart with joy. We have sought Your face, and now may the light of Your face shine upon us. Your smile sheds light, brightening these darkened days. With Your love like sunshine, and with heaven's music as a homing beacon, we walk in expectant joy. And the best is yet to come.

Then their eyes were opened and they recognized Him;
and...they said to one another,
  "Were not our hearts burning within us
  while He was speaking to us on the road,
  while He was explaining the Scriptures to us?" – Luke 24:31-32

We often walk through our days, unaware of Your presence. Surprise us by disclosing how near You have been to us all along. *Pray:*

- for the eyes of lost people to be opened so that they recognize the risen Jesus.

- for the Scriptures to be explained clearly, igniting hearts with hope and joy.

Seeking God for... **Military Personnel**

Pray for members of the military and their families who live in your city. Pray for the gospel to spread through the special relationships of military life; for wisdom as military personnel carry responsibilities in peace and in war; for grace upon chaplains and other spiritual leaders; that God will fortify families stretched by numerous moves and separations.

Prayerwalk: Pray near a military base or establishment.

A centurion came to Him, imploring Him... Now when Jesus heard this, He marveled, and said..."Truly I say to you, I have not found such great faith with anyone in Israel."

– Matthew 8:5, 10

...on behalf of the **Americas** *and the* **Caribbean**
United States of America, Uruguay, Venezuela, Virgin Islands of the USA

Seeking His KINGDOM
Christ's life on earth

For Christ to be served as King

When Jesus announced the kingdom of God He was declaring that God was fulfilling His purpose to subdue evil and bring people under the blessing of His Lordship.

To live on earth with the love of heaven

Jesus used the words "kingdom of God" to describe the soon-coming fulfillment of God's intention to gather a people from every people, forgiving their sin and filling them with power to live on earth with the love of heaven.

A mandate to pray

The coming of the kingdom is the advance of a great war against spiritual evil. Christ has already obtained utmost victory by His death and resurrection. He is now exalted as King of all heaven and earth. Because Christ is alive and at work accelerating the coming of God's kingly rule everywhere, we have a clear mandate to pray for outbreaks of His magnificent kingdom right here in our communities.

No kingless kingdom

God's kingdom is not a political agenda endorsed by Jesus. The kingdom is much more than a bundle of ethical maxims or economic ideals. The kingdom of Christ is all about what King Jesus Himself is doing and will accomplish. When people obey Jesus in simple trust and God-given love, the kingdom happens.

For the kingdom of God is… righteousness and peace and joy in the Holy Spirit.
– Romans 14:17

The Risen One presides right now

The Risen One, Jesus Himself, presides without coercion. He is patient – and yet He is passionate. He comes by invitation instead of by invasion into anyone's life.

Jesus is not seated in a box seat in heaven, watching at a distance as His followers struggle like gladiators with evil powers. Jesus works in our midst, a regal, glorious King. He has been given, and is now using, "all authority on heaven and earth" to fulfill all the Father has entrusted to Him. That's why Jesus taught us to pray for His kingdom to come on earth with all the beauty and power of heaven.

Praying for the King to come

For the rest of this 40-day season, we'll be seeking God to bring His kingdom. One specific way to pray for Christ's kingdom is to pray for the completion of what Christ began: the proclamation of the gospel of the kingdom. This next week we will begin by praying for the gospel of the kingdom to be clearly communicated to every people and place.

What God's kingdom looks like: righteousness, peace and joy

God's kingdom is not limited to what happens in church buildings. The life of Christ in His people can bring tangible changes in entire communities. Paul said that

"The kingdom of God is not a matter of eating and drinking, but of righteousness, peace and joy in the Holy Spirit." (Romans 14:17 NIV)

We will spend a week praying for each of these three things: righteousness, peace and joy. These things can only become a reality by the life and power of the Holy Spirit.

Jesus is patiently but passionately winning the great war against evil. We have a mandate to pray and labor with Him.

Seeking the GOSPEL of the KINGDOM

Christ is bringing the entire world under His Lordship. He is thwarting evil, liberating people and establishing outposts of heaven's life on earth. As people answer God's call to live as Christ's servants, they are changed, and they become God's agents to bring the blessings of Christ's Lordship to their communities.

Jesus said that the gospel of the kingdom would be proclaimed "in the whole world as a testimony to all the peoples" (Matthew 24:14). What wonderful hope: Every place. Every people. We can pray with confidence for the gospel to come to every geographical area and every cultural arena. Evangelization is the beginning point of all that God will do to bring forth His transforming blessing.

This gospel of the kingdom shall be proclaimed in the whole world as a testimony to all the peoples, and then the end will come.

– Matthew 24:14

This week we will extend our prayers for the peoples, cities, churches and families of Asia and the Pacific region.

Seeking God on behalf of **Asia** *and the* **Pacific**

to empower the proclaiming of His Word

Sunday
March 8

They will tell of the glory of Your kingdom and speak of Your might, so that all people may know of Your mighty acts and the glorious splendor of Your kingdom. – Psalm 145:11-12 NIV

You promised that a day will come when Your people will speak of Your kingdom with convincing clarity. The marvelous joy of living under Your Lordship will be seen and known. Fulfill this promise in our day and in our city. But we need more than better rhetoric to present Your power. How can mere words reveal the sweet reality of being loved and led by Jesus? Permeate our words with heaven's fragrance. Step out from the pages of the story and reveal the unique beauty of Your kingly rule.

––––––––––––––––––––––––

...as for you, go and proclaim everywhere the kingdom of God. – Luke 9:60

We sometimes count on professional preachers to evangelize our community. But even the best experts cannot connect with people in many arenas of our city. Give each one of us new courage to speak openly and often about the gospel of Your kingdom. *Pray:*

• for the gospel to be declared in every part of our city.

• for the King to be central in our talk about God's kingdom.

• that our lives and words would reveal the wonderful goodness of living under Christ's Lordship.

Seeking God for... Unemployed People

Pray that God will meet the needs of those without work in a way that they can clearly thank God for His provision; that they will soon find meaningful employment and glorify God for it; that God will open the way for righteous trade so that the entire city prospers in His provision.

Prayerwalk: Pray for those in your neighborhood who have recently lost their job or are struggling to find one.

That everyone may eat and drink, and find satisfaction in all his toil – this is the gift of God.
– Ecclesiastes 3:13 NIV

...on behalf of **Asia** *and the* **Pacific**

Afghanistan, American Samoa, Antarctica, Australia, Bangladesh, Bhutan, Brunei, Cambodia

Monday
March 9

to send His people to every place

Your descendants will...spread out
to the west and to the east and to the north and to the south.
And in you and in your descendants shall all the families of the earth be blessed.
　　　　　　　　　　　　　　　　　　　　　　　　　– Genesis 28:14

What You promised so long ago to our father Jacob has been partly fulfilled. Because Jesus rose from the dead, millions who believe in Him have been grafted into Jacob's faith family. And we are among them. But though we are many, we have yet to spread out to every place. Continue sending Your people to every place on earth. Send us to our own city so that the blessing of the gospel will be proclaimed in every circle and setting of our community. Make Your blessing visible so that wherever the gospel has been heard, it will also be seen in the lives of Your people. Establish tangible signs of Your ongoing goodness.

This gospel of the kingdom shall be proclaimed in the whole world
as a testimony to all the nations, and then the end will come. – Matthew 24:14

Equip everyday believers to be Your proclaimers. Support their testimony with clear demonstrations of Your love in the families and neighborhoods of our city. *Pray:*

- for Christians to labor together to finish the task of evangelizing the world.

- for the gospel to be conveyed clearly to overlooked groups in our city.

Let not the wise man boast of his wisdom or the strong man boast of his strength or the rich man boast of his riches, but let him who boasts boast about this: that he understands and knows Me.
– Jeremiah 9:23-24 NIV

Seeking God for...**Men**

Pray that men will seek God and honor Him in faithfulness, wisdom and truth; for their identity to be centered in Christ-like servant leadership; that the vision of their lives would be to serve and advance God's purposes.

Prayerwalk: Ask God to help you focus prayers of blessing on a few of the men that you see today.

...on behalf of **Asia** *and the* **Pacific**
China-People's Republic, China-Taiwan, Christmas Island, Cocos (Keeling) Islands, Cook Islands, Fiji

to rescue people enslaved in darkness

And I will appoint you as...a light to the nations,
to open blind eyes, to bring out prisoners from the dungeon
and those who dwell in darkness from the prison. – Isaiah 42:6-7

We know what it is like to be blinded by our own wrongdoing and to be held in spiritual bondage. Many in our city are trapped in patterns of sin that they cannot see. Come, Lord Jesus. You are the light of the world. Send Your light, to penetrate the darkness with brilliant healing power. Liberate those who are locked in darkness. Pry apart sealed eyelids. Illumine darkened minds. Wrench open prison doors. Cut the bonds that handcuff their hearts. Call each one to break free from what has bound them. May they follow You with grateful faithfulness.

Jesus said to them, "For a little while longer the Light is among you.
Walk while you have the Light, so that darkness will not overtake you."
– John 12:35

When people walk out of darkness into Your light, they are free to follow You. We pray today for those who are still in the twilight shadows, right on the verge of stepping into Your light and life. Call them to Yourself. Give them courage to follow You. *Pray:*

- for God to extend times of light, holding back the darkness, so that many more will follow Him.

- that those who see the light of Jesus will choose to follow Him and walk in His light.

Seeking God for...Health Care Workers

Pray that God will equip health care workers of every kind to serve with wise and loving hearts; that God will bless them with perseverance and joy; that the demands of their professions will bring no harm to their families and friendships; that many will follow Christ.

Prayerwalk: Pray on or near the grounds of a hospital, clinic or assisted living facility.

Blessed is he who has regard for the weak; the LORD delivers him in times of trouble.
The LORD will protect him and preserve his life; He will bless him in the land.
– Psalm 41:1-2 NIV

...on behalf of **Asia** *and the* **Pacific**
French Polynesia, Guam, Hong Kong, India, Indonesia, Japan, Kiribati

to reveal His glory by healing

They will see the glory of the LORD, the majesty of our God...
Say to those with anxious heart, "Take courage, fear not. Behold, your God will come"...
Then the eyes of the blind will be opened and the ears of the deaf will be unstopped.
Then the lame will leap like a deer, and the tongue of the mute will shout for joy.
— Isaiah 35:2, 4-6

Come to us in Your glory, mighty God. Dispel the cruel desperation of darkness – the foreboding sense that life is short, bleak and hopeless. Many are blinded by their sadness and deafened in despair. Restore their spiritual sight. Speak so they hear Your voice. As You heal, enable Your people to announce the amazing news: "Your God is coming! He is bringing His kingdom!" Unstopped ears will hear. Once-anxious hearts will exult in hope. May those who once were blind see Your soon-coming glory and rise to follow You.

Jesus was going throughout all Galilee...proclaiming the gospel of the kingdom, and healing every kind of disease and every kind of sickness among the people.
— Matthew 4:23

Give Your people bold expectations of Your coming kingdom. Move them to pray for sick people in the sincerity of Your love. Confirm the gospel with tangible demonstrations that You are as good as You are great. *Pray:*

- that Christians would pray with compassion for the sick as Jesus did.
- for the gospel of Christ's kingdom to be clearly conveyed by Your people as God displays His loving power through their prayers.

These are the things which you should do: speak the truth to one another; judge with truth and judgment for peace in your gates.
— Zechariah 8:16

Seeking God for...News and Media Workers

Pray for people throughout the industries of broadcast and print media to be strengthened in godly wisdom so that truth would be told and that attitudes of cynicism would be changed. Pray that productions would carry virtue and convey the values of Christ's kingdom.

Pray that many would come to know Christ.

Prayerwalk: Visit a media center, a broadcast station or a publisher of print media. Pray for the people working in these settings.

...on behalf of **Asia** *and the* **Pacific**

Korea-North, Korea-South, Laos, Macau, Malaysia, Maldives, Marshall Islands, Micronesia

to form new church communities

And He will arise and shepherd His flock in the strength of the LORD,
in the majesty of the name of the LORD His God...
at that time He will be great to the ends of the earth. – Micah 5:4

As it was written, so shall You be known in the last days. You are the long-expected Shepherd King. You will rise with zeal to bring about the greatest ingathering in all of history. No people on earth will be beyond Your reach. No power can withstand Your liberating love. We envision You, striding through the streets of our city, fearless and zealous, kind and patient – gentle as a shepherd, fearsome as a warrior. Find Your scattered, abandoned lambs. Guide them onward under Your Lordship. Make these new-found ones to be as one flock with many gatherings throughout our city.

The Lord...sent them in pairs ahead of Him to every city and place
where He Himself was going to come. And He was saying...
"Go. Behold, I send you out as lambs in the midst of wolves." – Luke 10:1-3

Come to every part of our city. We welcome You, mighty Shepherd. Send us ahead of You to prepare Your way by prayer. Keep us weak like sheep so that Your power is on display to those who oppose You. Gather many to Your flock by the power of the gospel. *Pray:*

- for Your people to bring the gospel to every neighborhood, gathering believers together in every part of the city.

- for Christ's flock to display His character in the midst of opposition.

Seeking God for...**the Unborn**

Pray that these children will be acknowledged and honored by all; for them to find sheltering homes and loving families; that the awful waste of their lives would cease; that God would turn the hearts of the parents of unborn babies toward their children.

Prayerwalk: As you walk through your neighborhood pray that God will give people a heart and a lifestyle of love and honor for children of any age. Pray for God's healing for any who may have harmed their children in any way.

For He will deliver...the afflicted who have no one to help. He will... save the needy from death. He will rescue them from oppression and violence, for precious is their blood in His sight.
– Psalm 72:12-14 NIV

...on behalf of **Asia** *and the* **Pacific**

Mongolia, Myanmar, Nauru, Nepal, New Caledonia, New Zealand, Niue, Norfolk Island

Friday
March 13

to advance citywide movements

It will yet be that peoples will come, even the inhabitants of many cities.
The inhabitants of one will go to another, saying,
   "Let us go at once to entreat the favor of the LORD,
   and to seek the LORD of hosts; I will also go."
So many peoples and mighty nations will come to seek the LORD of hosts.
                                                    – Zechariah 8:20-22

Set off chain reactions that will roll throughout our community. Move one person to tell another, who will then tell someone else, so that people all over our city get a fresh hearing of the gospel. Many have been seeking You privately. Stir their hearts to influence many more to seek You openly. Cause the curious to become seekers, and the seekers to become leaders. Instigate movements through networks and neighborhoods. Accelerate the spread of gospel talk through the markets of business, the places of entertainment and the halls of government.

When the entire crowd saw Him, they were amazed,
and began running up to greet Him.   *– Mark 9:15*

We pray for groups of people, small and large, to encounter You together. When people realize what You have done for them and for others, they recognize who You really are. The wonder and awe will draw many more to seek You eagerly. *Pray:*

   • for Jesus to amaze people by what He does, but also to be trusted for who He is.

   • for circles of friends, work groups in business and classmates in schools to encounter Jesus together.

Since my youth, O God,
you have taught me,
and to this day
I declare Your
marvelous deeds.
   – Psalm 71:17 NIV

Seeking God for...**University Students**

Pray for students to follow Christ; for gospel truth to be proclaimed in settings that are often hostile and cynical toward matters of faith. Pray for students to make wise decisions and shape their careers and ambitions to fulfill God's global purposes.

Pray for strong leadership among Christian groups on campuses; for the advance of movements of prayer and mission mobilization.

Prayerwalk: Pray for students at a place of higher education.

...on behalf of **Asia** *and the* **Pacific**

Northern Mariana Islands, Pakistan, Palau, Papua New Guinea, Philippines, Samoa, Singapore, Solomon Islands

SEEKING GOD...

for Him to be famous for His works

May His name increase as long as the sun shines...
Blessed be the LORD God, the God of Israel, who alone works wonders.
And blessed be His glorious name forever.
And may the whole earth be filled with His glory. — Psalm 72:17-19

Despite the goodness You always show to everyone, You are not recognized throughout our city. Become known beyond the walls of our church buildings. Be anonymous no longer. Make Yourself famous for who You truly are. As prayers in Your name are answered, as the gospel of Your kingdom is clearly declared, and as You are openly praised as Lord, flood our city with the light of Your glory. Your glory shines as once-broken families rejoice in rekindled love, or when addicted ones break free from debilitating habits, or when depressed ones lift buoyant hearts again with joy. May the reports of such praise-worthy wonders fill our community with Your glory, like a slow, steady sunrise.

"But for this purpose I came to this hour. Father, glorify Your name."
Then a voice came out of heaven:
"I have both glorified it, and will glorify it again." — John 12:27-28

Father, glorify Yourself. You have done it many times before. You have promised that You will do it again. *Pray:*

- for Christians to live for the same purpose for which Jesus lived: for God to be openly glorified.

- for God to be recognized and thanked as He transforms peoples' lives by the power of the gospel.

Seeking God for...**Refugees**

Pray for immigration to take place legally and honorably. Pray for protection and provision. Pray for families to be reunited and for those desiring to return to homelands to be granted temporary asylum and swift repatriation. Pray for Christians to open their homes and neighborhoods in wise and helpful ways. Pray for the gospel to be heard, drawing many to Christ.

Prayerwalk: Pray prayers of blessing and protection for refugees and immigrants in your community.

He defends the cause of the fatherless and the widow, and loves the alien, giving him food and clothing. And you are to love those who are aliens, for you yourselves were aliens in Egypt.
— Deuteronomy 10:18-19 NIV

...on behalf of **Asia** *and the* **Pacific**

Sri Lanka, Thailand, Tibet, Timor Leste, Tonga, Tuvalu, Vanuatu, Vietnam, Wallis and Futuna

Seeking the RIGHTEOUSNESS of His KINGDOM

Our society is at war with the idea that there is virtue, purity or moral excellence. Those who consider themselves to be living rightly are thought to be condemning all others as wrong. But our God loves righteousness. Originally, He created everything with beauty and order – a "rightness" which has been warped by sin. Ultimately He will bring a new heaven and a new earth "in which righteousness dwells" (2 Peter 3:13).

God desires to bring a measure of righteousness in our communities in our day. The reality of righteousness is always related to justice. We will pray for King Jesus to press forward His war against evil in tangible ways, liberating those who are oppressed. Christ is saving people, whether their affliction is a result of their own wrong choices or the injustice of others. Christ teaches that we are to seek His kingdom, and with it, His righteousness.

The sun of righteousness will rise with healing in its wings.

– Malachi 4:2

This week we will be praying for the cities, peoples, tribes and countries of the continent of Africa.

Seeking God on behalf of **Africa**

to bring forth justice in the city

Sunday
March 15

Behold, My Servant, whom I uphold;
My chosen one in whom My soul delights.
I have put My Spirit upon Him.
He will bring forth justice to the nations.
He will not cry out or raise His voice, nor make His voice heard in the street...
He will faithfully bring forth justice. He will not be disheartened or crushed
until He has established justice in the earth. — Isaiah 42:1-4

You send Your Servant to the cities of the earth. We may have ignored Him, but He has long been at work and He will never stop. He has outlasted every compromised king and every corrupt judge. He is heaven's chosen one, mantled with the Spirit of God. He has been charged to bring forth justice, and He will not fail. We may have overlooked Him because He does not campaign among the rich. Nor does He foment revolution among the poor. Instead He is a healing leader, transforming the weak to become like Him. We pray for His mission to be accomplished in our city. Let us be found with Him, serving among the forgotten and broken. Put His Spirit upon us as well so that we can labor with Him faithfully in hope.

I tell you that He will bring about justice for them quickly.
However, when the Son of Man comes, will He find faith on the earth? — Luke 18:8

Will You find faith on the earth? The answer is Yes! When You come You will find many of us believing You with our prayers and our actions.
Pray:

• for God to bring forth justice for those who are abused.

• for Christians to pray and labor with persistent faith.

Seeking God for... International Visitors

Pray for students, workers and businesspeople from other lands to be treated with honor and respect; that they will enjoy new friendships; that they will encounter the message of the gospel clearly declared and lovingly demonstrated.

Prayerwalk: Find a public place or business which draws international visitors or students. As you see people from different nations, pray God's blessing on them and their home countries.

Assemble the people — men, women and children, and the aliens living in your towns — so they can listen and learn to fear the LORD your God.
— Deuteronomy 31:12 NIV

...on behalf of **Africa**
Angola, Benin, Botswana, Burkina Faso, Burundi, Cameroon, Cape Verde Islands

Monday
March 16

to forgive unrighteousness

Righteousness belongs to You, O Lord, but...open shame belongs to us...
our princes and our fathers, because we have sinned against You.
Open Your eyes and see our desolations...
O Lord, hear! O Lord, forgive! O Lord, listen and take action!
For Your own sake, O my God, do not delay,
because Your city and Your people are called by Your name! – Daniel 9:7-8, 18-19

People throughout our city have suffered in the aftermath of wrongs committed by others. We could excuse ourselves, claiming that we have done no wrong. But we make our appeal to You now, as if we were standing alongside every person of our community. We identify with those who have been abused, and also with those who have brought harm. We confess our unrighteousness as a people. Forgive us! Help us! We ask You to act in Your boundless compassion. But we can also ask You to act for Your own sake. Since Your name and reputation is carried by so many of our city, we ask that You would act for the glory of Your name!

And they brought to Him a paralytic lying on a bed. Seeing their faith,
Jesus said to the paralytic, "Take courage, son; your sins are forgiven." – Matthew 9:2

The displayed faith of a few people moved You to forgive the sins of their friend. Look now on our city, Lord Jesus, as we bring our community to You, one friend at a time. Bring forgiveness. *Pray:*

- for believers to pray with faith for people far from God.

- for Christ's forgiveness to free those paralyzed by their sin.

> *But God, who comforts the downcast, comforted us.*
> – 2 Corinthians 7:6 NIV

Seeking God for... **Depressed People**

Pray for helpful counsel and hope-building relationships; for the healing of long-standing wounds of mind and soul; that the light of gospel truth will dispel the lies and oppressive power of Satan; for the comfort and hope of the Holy Spirit renewing their minds in Christ.

Prayerwalk: Pray for people you see today who may be downcast, even though they might appear to be cheerful and strong.

...on behalf of **Africa**

Central African Republic, Chad, Comoros, Congo-Democratic Republic (Zaire), Côte d'Ivoire, Djibouti

for the gift of righteousness

Tuesday
March 17

Behold, as for the proud one, his soul is not right within him;
but the righteous will live by his faith.   – Habakkuk 2:4

Our self-justifying pride has warped us. The straight edges inside our souls are ruined. We lose track of what is good or evil. We neglect to check ourselves against Your righteousness. Help us. Straighten what is twisted in our arrogant hearts. Grant to us the one thing that will renew us to live rightly: the gift of faith. Give us faith to live in hourly reliance upon You instead of trusting ourselves in foolish pride. We pray for others in our city, that they too will come to meet Christ and live by trusting Him. May they experience the clean sweetness of God-wrought humility and righteousness.

When the disciples heard this, they were very astonished and said,
"Then who can be saved?" And looking at them Jesus said to them,
"With people this is impossible, but with God all things are possible."
    – Matthew 19:25-26

Mighty Savior, do the impossible: Save us from our self-sufficiency. Our wealth, knowledge and good deeds too easily deceive us. Keep calling the rich and the religious, as well as the poor and powerless, who often find it hard to trust You. *Pray:*

- for many among intellectuals, the wealthy, the religious and the powerful to hear and to respond to Christ's call.

- for God to grant the saving gift of trusting Christ for His righteousness.

Seeking God for...**Fathers**

Pray that fathers will serve and care for their families, that absentee fathers would change their lifestyles to nurture their wives and children; that children will see the character of the heavenly Father in the lives of their dads.

Prayerwalk: Pray for the fathers or grandfathers in your workplace or near your home.

Fathers, do not exasperate your children; instead, bring them up in the training and instruction of the Lord.
– Ephesians 6:4 NIV

...on behalf of **Africa**

Equatorial Guinea, Eritrea, Ethiopia, Gabon, Gambia, Ghana, Guinea, Guinea-Bissau

Wednesday
March 18

to give leaders love for truth

Behold, a king will reign righteously and princes will rule justly...
Then the eyes of those who see will not be blinded,
and the ears of those who hear will listen.
The mind of the rash will come to discern the truth...
No longer will the fool be called noble...   – Isaiah 32:1, 3-5

We pray for our leaders, that they will seek truth, and thus come to pursue righteousness in our community. Make them ambitious to do what is right because they love what is true. Surround our leaders with people of character. Give them courage to ignore those who claim to be wise, but do what is false or foolish. Bestow the wisdom of Christ-like integrity to all who govern, teach, judge or counsel. May they bring forth genuine justice based on truth.

Therefore Pilate said to Him, "So You are a king?" Jesus answered,
"You say correctly that I am a king. For this I have been born,
and for this I have come into the world, to testify to the truth. Everyone who is
of the truth hears My voice." Pilate said to Him, "What is truth?"   – John 18:37-38

King Jesus, challenge the leaders of our land to love truth more than power. Make them aware of the greater purpose that they serve in their spheres of leadership. Call them to be lovers and leaders of truth. *Pray:*

• for Christ to meet the cynical with truth and the searching with hope.

• for Jesus to reveal His kingship to leaders at every level.

• for those who sincerely seek the truth to hear the voice of Jesus.

But remember the LORD your God, for it is He who gives you the ability to produce wealth.
– Deuteronomy 8:18 NIV

Seeking God for...**Business People**

Ask God to bless those who base business practices in righteousness. Pray that God will prosper those who pursue their business as mission for God's kingdom. Pray for the gospel to spread in the marketplace; for righteous managers and executives; for creative, godly entrepreneurs.

Prayerwalk: As you pass through a place of business today, pray for Christ to be followed and for His name to be honored in that setting. Pray for God to bless the endeavors that exemplify His kingdom.

...on behalf of **Africa**
Kenya, Lesotho, Liberia, Madagascar, Malawi, Mali, Mauritania, Mauritius

*How long will the enemy mock You, O God? Will the foe revile Your name forever?
...Have regard for Your covenant, because haunts of violence fill the dark places of the land.
Do not let the oppressed retreat in disgrace. May the poor and needy praise Your name.
Rise up, O God, and defend Your cause.* – Psalm 74:10, 20-22 NIV

In many cities of our land, the numbers of righteous men and women have dwindled. Within this lawless void, cruel and dominating powers have risen, shattering covenant love and trust. Innocent people are trapped in the crossfire of violence and crime. We ask You to intervene on behalf of the afflicted. Subdue evil powers which amplify anger and energize greed. Break the cycle of escalating revenge and hatred. Rise up, O God. You are Judge of all the earth. Restrain the insidious evil that has darkened our land. Protect the place of the righteous. Be their defense. Turn many to trust in You. Cause them to become Your agents of forgiveness and light.

"And this woman...whom Satan has bound for eighteen long years, should she not have been released from this bond on the Sabbath day?" As He said this, all His opponents were being humiliated; and the entire crowd was rejoicing over all the glorious things being done by Him. – Luke 13:16-17

Release those who suffer in the grip of Satan's power. Humiliate those who oppose You by doing great things that bring You great praise. *Pray:*

• for Christ to be glorified as He liberates people oppressed by dark powers.

• For God to bring righteousness to our city, breaking the tyranny of satanic power.

*Seeking God for...***Agricultural Workers**

Pray that God will bless families who farm, ranch or support agricultural industries, that they would prosper. Pray that they would follow Christ and find ways to be part of life-giving churches. Pray especially for migrant workers who sometimes face injustice and difficulties.

Prayerwalk: Pray in a rural area for God's blessing on the land and the families that He has placed there.

The LORD your God will bless you in all your produce and in all the work of your hands, so that you will be altogether joyful.
– Deuteronomy 16:15

...on behalf of **Africa**
Mayotte, Mozambique, Namibia, Niger, Nigeria, Republic of Congo, Réunion

DAY 24

SEEKING GOD...

Friday
March 20

for courage to contend
for righteousness

The LORD reigns, let the earth rejoice...
His lightnings lit up the world. The earth saw and trembled.
The mountains melted like wax...at the presence of the Lord of the whole earth.
The heavens declare His righteousness, and all the peoples have seen His glory...
Hate evil, you who love the LORD, who preserves the souls of His godly ones...
Light is sown like seed for the righteous and gladness for the upright in heart.
– Psalm 97:1, 4-6, 10-11

You will come like a lightning blast at the final hour, lighting up the world with mountain-melting judgment. Your judgment will be so perfect and so powerful that the earth won't know whether to tremble or to cheer. We delight in Your wondrous judgment. Give us ears to hear the heavens sing of the glory of Your righteousness. Give us eyes to see You even now confronting evil and setting things right. Sprinkle bits of the last-day lightning in our hearts, as if You were planting seeds of light. Cause these seeds to sprout like living hope, strengthening Your people to stand against evil, to work for justice and to welcome Your coming day.

Now He was telling them a parable to show that at all times
they ought to pray and not to lose heart. *– Luke 18:1*

Some of us have lost hope that You will bring forth justice before the end of the age. Give us stalwart hearts to pursue the prayers of Your righteous purpose until You come. *Pray:*

• for Christ to encourage those weary in the struggle for righteousness.

• for Christians to be persistent and patient in crying out for justice.

Let the little children come to Me, and do not hinder them, for the kingdom of God belongs to such as these.
– Mark 10:14 NIV

Seeking God for...**Children**

Pray that children will hear the gospel and encounter Christ early in life; that God's fatherly heart will be revealed to kids, especially to those who may have been wounded or disappointed by their parents; for family stability; for excellence in education; for wisdom to be formed in their early years; for safety from perversion and violence.

Prayerwalk: Pray for kids in your neighborhood or pray near schools and playgrounds in any part of town. Pray for the entire family that surrounds the children that you see.

...on behalf of **Africa**

Rwanda, Saint Helena, São Tomé and Príncipe, Senegal, Seychelles, Sierra Leone, Somalia, South Africa

to guide many
in lives of righteousness

Saturday
March 21

God be gracious to us and bless us, and cause His face to shine upon us...
Let the peoples praise You, O God! Let all the peoples praise You!
Let the nations be glad and sing for joy; for You will judge the peoples
with uprightness and guide the nations on the earth. — Psalm 67:1, 3-4

Never have You been more praised across the face of the earth. Every year, You are worshiped in more languages. Every day, thousands begin to follow You for the first time. In our city You are loved now only by a portion of the many who will eventually turn to You. We praise You today in anticipation of some of the greatest works that You will ever do in history. Fulfill Your promise to be gracious and to bless people in every place. Accomplish Your promise to intervene as a mighty, righteous judge. Thwart every kind of evil. Begin to set things right. As a magnificent King, show people from every nation how to follow You with lives of righteousness.

Now judgment is upon this world; now the ruler of this world will be cast out.
And I, if I am lifted up from the earth, will draw all people to Myself. — John 12:31-32

Lord Jesus, Your death began the judgment of Satan, launching a regime change on the earth. We ask that You would bring the power of Your cross and resurrection against evil powers in our city. Be exalted by Your people and draw many more to follow You. *Pray:*

- for God to overcome the powers of darkness that hold people in bondage.

- for the resurrected Lord to be exalted in our community so that He draws many people to Himself.

Seeking God for... **Gangs**

Pray that God will satisfy gang members' desires for belonging and significance; for God to break the spiritual and social powers that hold them; for caring Christians to embrace them in the authentic love of God's family; for blessing upon the neighborhoods they claim.

Prayerwalk: Pray at or near a place affected by gang activity. Speak words of truth from the Bible to spiritually "tag" the territories with unseen but real declarations of Christ's Lordship, love and blessing.

Help, LORD, for the godly man ceases to be, for the faithful disappear from among the sons of men... "Now I will arise," says the LORD, "I will set him in the safety for which he longs."
— Psalm 12:1, 5

...on behalf of **Africa**

South Sudan, Sudan, Swaziland, Tanzania, Togo, Uganda, Western Sahara, Zambia, Zimbabwe

Seeking the PEACE of His KINGDOM

Peace in our cities seems like the empty wishes of politicians and beauty queens. In fact, our Lord promised that wars and strife would increase. The Scriptures however, call us to pray for peace and aspire to be peacemakers. How then does God want us to pray for peace?

God desires to bring outbreaks of peace right in the midst of the worst troubles of our world. This week our focus is praying for the peace of Christ's kingdom. Every time Jesus heals a relationship, reconciles embattled families, or restores respect and honor among races, He is demonstrating His coming kingdom. Fresh manifestations of peace send a signal that He will eventually overwhelm evil and reconcile the world to Himself. For His glory we will seek God to bring His kingdom to our homes, neighborhoods, cities and countries in His peacemaking power.

Behold, I extend peace to her like a river.
– Isaiah 66:12

This fourth week we will direct our prayers with and for the people, churches and countries of Europe and Central Asia.

Seeking God on behalf of **Europe** *and* **Central Asia**

to declare His peace among the nations

Behold, your king is coming to you; He is just and endowed with salvation, humble, and mounted on a donkey...
I will cut off the chariot...and the bow of war will be cut off.
And He will speak peace to the nations. — Zechariah 9:9-10

Come, long-awaited Messiah. One day You will suddenly break through the heavens, and every eye will see You. But before that great day, we pray that You would be received as the King that You are. Visit our cities, bringing Your rule by the power of the gospel. You alone can lift Your voice and say the word "Peace!" as a command. Speak with Your kingly authority into the turmoil of the peoples striving against each other. Calm the storms of hostility by bringing many under Your Lordship. You alone can disarm our terrorized hearts and demilitarize our lives. Announce Your peace to the nations. Even so, come, King Jesus! Preside over us as our Savior-King.

Peace I leave with you; My peace I give to you; not as the world gives do I give to you.
Do not let your heart be troubled, nor let it be fearful. — John 14:27

We know how to create quickly passing moods of tranquility. But Your peace is different. May Your peace be upon us – a peace that heals troubled hearts and relationships, forbidding us to fear.
Pray:

- for the peace of Jesus to be proclaimed to troubled hearts and homes.

- for Jesus to give His peace to those who have not yet known Him, vanquishing fears and imparting new hope.

Seeking God for...**Government Leaders**

Pray that they will be examples of righteousness in our society; that they will experience God's wisdom in their deliberations; that they will speak and carry out dealings with truth; that they will not hinder the service and worship of Jesus Christ; that they will come to know, honor and follow Christ.

Prayerwalk: Visit a center of city, county, state or federal government. Pray on or near the site. Leave a short note for a particular official which describes your prayers for God to bless him or her.

I urge, then, first of all, that requests, prayers, intercession and thanksgiving be made for everyone – for kings and all those in authority.
— 1 Timothy 2:1-2 NIV

...on behalf of **Europe** and **Central Asia**
Albania, Andorra, Armenia, Austria, Azerbaijan, Belarus, Belgium, Bosnia and Herzegovina, Bulgaria

to instruct us in His ways of peace

And many peoples will come and say,
"Come, let us go up to the mountain of the Lord...
that He may teach us concerning His ways"...
And they will hammer their swords into plowshares...
Nation will not lift up sword against nation, and never again will they learn war.

– Isaiah 2:3-4

Unceasing war surrounds us. But we believe Your promise that the nations will rush to You, "unlearning" ways of war in order to finally live in peace. You are the same God today that You will be on the last day. It is not too early for the nations to be changed by Your teaching. Transform us now by training us in Your ways. Empower Your people to accomplish Your will by giving and forgiving. Impart to us the power of life-giving blessing. Most of all, teach us how You love, so that the people of our city will see the coming peace of Your kingdom.

He was teaching in the temple...And all the people would get up early
in the morning to come to Him in the temple to listen to Him.   – Luke 21:37-38

Lord Jesus, we ask for great movements of people of our city to seek You, to hear Your word and to follow in Your ways. *Pray:*

• for Jesus' teaching to be creatively conveyed in life-changing ways.

• for people to experience the peace-making power of Christ's teaching.

Be shepherds of God's flock that is under your care...Cast all your anxiety on Him because He cares for you.

– 1 Peter 5:2, 7 NIV

Seeking God for...**Pastors**

Pray that pastors and church leaders will be filled with wisdom; that they will be honored by those they serve; that God will pour His Spirit upon them in power and humility, giving fresh intimacy with Jesus; for protection from the plots of the evil one against their families; that deep friendships with other pastors will grow.

Prayerwalk: Pray outside a church building for the pastor(s) who serve(s) that church.

...on behalf of **Europe** *and* **Central Asia**

Canary Islands, Croatia, Czech Republic, Denmark, Estonia, Faeroe Islands, Finland

to heal broken relationships

*"Please forgive the transgression of the servants of the God of your father."
And Joseph wept when they spoke to him...But Joseph said to them,
"Do not be afraid, for am I in God's place? As for you, you meant evil against me,
but God meant it for good in order to bring about this present result..."*

– Genesis 50:17, 19-20

One wrongdoing always seems to bring about another. Minor tiffs can provoke vindictive, never-ending feuds. Only the power of forgiveness can break cycles of vengeance and fear. We believe that You, the God of all goodness, can turn around the schemes of evil intent, in order to bring forth the triumph of all that is good. Cause our hearts to move in Your mercy, so that forgiveness flows, healing the horrific aftermath of sin. By the Christ-like forgiveness of a few, bring a greater goodness for many.

...when the doors were shut where the disciples were, for fear...Jesus came and stood in their midst and said to them..."Peace be with you; as the Father has sent Me, I also send you." And when He had said this, He breathed on them and said to them, "Receive the Holy Spirit. If you forgive the sins of any, their sins have been forgiven them..."   *– John 20:19-23*

Fear of retaliation and shame can close the doors of our hearts. Break in and breathe upon us. Break the stalemate of broken relationships with Your peace. Authorize us to forgive by the power of Your Spirit. *Pray:*

- for God to flip plots for evil to advance His purpose for good.

- for Christ to bring a wave of forgiveness in our city, penetrating barricades of fear, softening hearts and mending relationships.

Seeking God for... Native Peoples

Pray for native peoples who live in or near your city to be honored for who they are and for all God intends them to be. Pray for God to heal any harm that may have come from broken treaties and mistreatment; that they will experience dignity and justice; that churches will flourish among them and that God's praise will resound in native languages.

Prayerwalk: As you prayerwalk in your neighborhood, consider the native peoples who first dwelled in the area that has become your city. Pray for their descendants.

> *Let the nations be glad and sing for joy; for You will judge the peoples with uprightness and guide the nations on the earth.*
>
> *– Psalm 67:4*

...on behalf of Europe *and* Central Asia

France, Georgia, Germany, Gibraltar, Greece, Hungary, Iceland, Ireland

Wednesday
March 25

for the homecoming of many prodigals

Lift up your eyes round about and see.
They all gather together, they come to you.
Your sons will come from afar, and your daughters will be carried in the arms.
Then you will see and be radiant, and your heart will thrill and rejoice...   – Isaiah 60:4-5

We await Your promise that many lost sons and daughters will be called back home. We have kept watch with those who are bereft of loved ones. We have grown weary in the watching for signs of their return. But if You lift our hearts, we will lift our eyes in hope. Your voice can summon them home from self-imposed exile. We pray for an early sign of this end-time homecoming to be seen in our broken homes. We mention the names of prodigal children, and even runaway wives and husbands. Bring them home to You. Carry them on Your shoulders. Gather our families again. Reconcile children to their parents. Heal our marriages. Fill our homes with Your abiding presence.

So he got up and came to his father. But while he was still
a long way off, his father saw him and felt compassion for him,
and ran and embraced him and kissed him.   – Luke 15:20

Call our wayward children home. Give them the yearning and resolve to return to You and to their families. *Pray:*

• for prodigals to begin their journey home to God.

• for Christians to show God's compassion to those who have broken fellowship with God, and to welcome them home.

He has filled him with the Spirit of God, with skill, ability and knowledge in all kinds of crafts...to engage in all kinds of artistic craftsmanship.
– Exodus 35:31, 33 NIV

Seeking God for...**Arts** and **Entertainment**

Pray that God will inspire artists and entertainers with creativity and wisdom that reflect God's beauty; that they will seek God and come to follow Christ with courage; that their work will bring strength, goodness and hope to our communities.

Prayerwalk: Visit an art museum, a theater or a place of entertainment for the purpose of praying for the artists or those working in support capacities.

...on behalf of **Europe** and **Central Asia**

Italy, Kazakhstan, Kosovo, Kyrgyzstan, Latvia, Liechtenstein, Lithuania, Luxembourg

for the rebuilding of devastated cities

Thursday
March 26

And the LORD will continually guide you, and satisfy your desire in scorched places...
You will be like a watered garden, and like a spring of water whose waters do not fail. ...
You will rebuild the ancient ruins...You will be called the repairer of the breach,
the restorer of the streets in which to dwell. – Isaiah 58:11-12

Our cities are blighted by broken relationships, bringing either endless enmity or dismal apathy. Deeds of kindness seem to be wasted, as if we are planting gardens in dry sand dunes. Come upon us, mighty Creator. Open springs in our souls, coursing with the life-bringing power of the Resurrected One. Stir us to yearn again for a transformed city. Bring on the long-promised generation who will be honored to become rebuilders of broken relationships. Heal what is shattered. Clear away the rubble. Remake the spiritual foundations so that our city becomes known as a place where families and many peoples flourish, a place where You will be delighted to dwell.

Whatever house you enter, first say, "Peace be to this house." If a man of peace is there,
your peace will rest on him; but if not, it will return to you. – Luke 10:5-6

Raise up people of peace. Enable them to lead others who learn to love and grow in Your ways. May they become foundations of a renewed city. *Pray:*

- for Christ to establish embassies of His peace and His kingdom in every neighborhood of our city.

- for influential men and women to become dedicated Christ followers.

Seeking God for... the Athletic Industry

Pray that God will reveal His calling and purpose for the students and coaches in high school, university and professional programs. Pray for those in support roles and those with higher profiles, that they will know Christ and fulfill God's calling in their lives. Pray that **athletes would live with integrity and act responsibly with wealth and reputation.**

Prayerwalk: Pray on-site at the place of an upcoming sports event near you.

Yours, O LORD, is the greatness and the power and the glory... Wealth and honor come from You...In Your hands are strength and power to exalt and give strength to all.
– 1 Chronicles 29:11-12 NIV

...on behalf of **Europe** *and* **Central Asia**

Macedonia, Malta, Moldova, Monaco, Montenegro, Netherlands, Norway, Poland, Portugal

Friday
March 27

to raise up peacemakers by His Spirit

The Spirit of the LORD will rest on Him,
   the spirit of wisdom and understanding,
   the spirit of counsel and strength,
   the spirit of knowledge and the fear of the LORD.   – Isaiah 11:2

Put Your Spirit of peacemaking power upon Your people – the same Spirit that empowered the work of Jesus. Give us the Spirit of wisdom and understanding, so that many will grasp Your ways and walk in Your light. Give us the Spirit of counsel and strength, that we might bring healing by our words and impart stamina to others so that they persevere in hope. Give us the Spirit of knowledge and the fear of the Lord so that we may help many to walk in the joyous awe of knowing You – and being known by You. By Your Spirit raise us up to be champions of change. Make us mighty in meekness to wage Your peace so that our city exhibits the life of Your coming kingdom.

Blessed are the peacemakers, for they shall be called sons of God.   – Matthew 5:9

May Your people instill hope for restored relationships in the midst of family feuds and racial tensions. By their lives and counsel, bring reconciling grace into families, workplaces and neighborhoods. *Pray:*

- for gifted, Christ-like people to serve as mediators in strife-torn homes and neighborhoods.

- for people of different churches to form new relationships of unity.

O LORD, You have heard the desire of the humble. You will strengthen their heart. You will incline Your ear to vindicate the orphan and the oppressed.

– Psalm 10:17-18

Seeking God for...Orphans

Pray for children who have lost their parents, or who are now in foster care away from their birth parents; for safe, loving, permanent homes with godly adoptive or foster parents; for healing from effects of physical, emotional or sexual abuse; for siblings to be adopted together; for those who have "aged out" of adoptive services, that they will find wise mentors and a secure place in the family of God.

Prayerwalk: Pray for people in your neighborhood who God may be calling to become foster or adoptive parents. Pray that they will act in His love and wisdom.

...on behalf of **Europe** *and* **Central Asia**

Romania, Russia, San Marino, Serbia, Slovakia, Slovenia, Spain, Sweden

to fill our city with heaven's peace

The LORD...will fill Zion with justice and righteousness.
He will be the sure foundation for your times,
a rich store of salvation and wisdom and knowledge;
the fear of the LORD is the key to this treasure.
Look, their brave men cry aloud in the streets; the envoys of peace weep bitterly...
The treaty is broken, its witnesses are despised, no one is respected. – Isaiah 33:5-8 NIV

The leaders of our land try to suppress the worst violence. But despite lulls in conflict, crime and cruelty continue. We cannot bring forth the dignity and honor of city-wide peace in any lasting way. Our leaders express our sorrow, but they cannot hide their discouragement and fear that darker days will come. And so we appeal to You, King Jesus. Overflow our city from the reservoirs of peace that fill heaven. May the fear of God become a key that unlocks for us the great treasure of Your heart. Cause heaven's wealth to cascade down upon us. Fill our minds with knowledge. Fill our hearts with wisdom. Fill our agendas with redemption. And fill our city with peace like a river.

He saw the city and wept over it, saying, "If you had known in this day, even you,
the things which make for peace! But now they have been hidden from your eyes."
– Luke 19:41-42

As You gaze upon our city, we stand and weep with You. Open our eyes to recognize Your ways and Your work to bring about city-wide peace. *Pray:*

- for our hearts to grieve, along with Christ, the daily devastation of peace-deprived lives in our community.
- that Christ will form true peace amidst families, neighbors and co-workers.

Seeking God for...**Women**

Pray for women to be honored in their God-created glory; that every kind of injustice toward women will cease; for pornography to be stopped; for protection from sexual violence; that hope would be renewed **for the beauty of marriage and children; that single women would lay hold of God's full purpose in their lives.**

Prayerwalk: Pray prayers of blessing for some of the women you come in contact with today.

This woman was abounding with deeds of kindness and charity which she continually did.
– Acts 9:36

...*on behalf of* **Europe** *and* **Central Asia**

Switzerland, Tajikistan, Turkmenistan, Ukraine, United Kingdom, Uzbekistan, Vatican City

Seeking the JOY of the KINGDOM

How can we pray in faith for joy amidst the furies of war, injustice and fearsome epidemics? Whenever people walk together under the Lordship of Christ, true joy can abound. As people experience Christ's coming kingdom, there can be growing joy as the Holy Spirit reveals the incredible sweetness and substance of what is to come. The joy of His kingdom is a "sneak preview" of the coming attractions of heaven happening now on earth.

Joy is different than happiness – pleasant feelings that depend on agreeable circumstances. The joy of Christ, however, is an abiding reality, formed and revealed by the Holy Spirit. Since Christ's kingdom of joy is coming, it's time to get the party started. The celebration of a few can brighten an entire community.

*They will come
and shout for joy...
and their life
will be like
a watered garden.*

– Jeremiah 31:12

During this fifth week, our prayers will be focused on the peoples, churches and countries of the Middle East.

Seeking God on behalf of the **Middle East**

for the joy of hope in times of trouble

Sunday
March 29

*God is our refuge and strength, a very present help in trouble.
    Therefore we will not fear, though the earth should change
    and though the mountains slip into the heart of the sea...
There is a river whose streams make glad the city of God,
    the holy dwelling places of the Most High. God is in the midst of her,
    she will not be moved; God will help her when morning dawns.*   – Psalm 46:1-2, 4-5

Many still remember when terror was rare, as unexpected as an earthquake. But now, random violence is relentless. It is hard not to fear that all that is solid and sure might soon dissolve into chaos. You, the Most High, are not far, but altogether present in the midst of Your people. Give us sanctuary in the certainty of Your presence. Be our refuge. Become our strength. Give us steady streams of gladness in Your nearness and goodness. Cause many in our city to see the soon-coming dawn of Your kingdom.

These things I speak in the world so that they may have My joy made full in themselves.
                                                                    – John 17:13

Lord Jesus, You are now at the Father's right hand. But You make Your voice heard to those who listen. Cause Your voice to be heard so that many will experience Your joy. *Pray:*

• for people to find joy in taking refuge in God.

• that those who have only known the hollow cheer of worldly pleasures would hear Christ's voice and experience genuine joy.

Seeking God for... Homeless People

Pray for immediate relief, shelter, food and health care; that Christ will restore hope for the future; for wise counsel and trustworthy friendships; for protection from the risks of life on the streets; for employment, housing and restored family life.

Prayerwalk: Visit a place where homeless people seek shelter or employment. Pray God's blessing on people you see who appear to be homeless.

But He lifted the needy out of their affliction and increased their families like flocks.
    – Psalm 107:41 NIV

...on behalf of the **Middle East**

Algeria, Bahrain, Cyprus

Monday
March 30
for the joy of liberation

When the LORD brought back the captive ones of Zion,
*   we were like those who dream.*
Then our mouth was filled with laughter and our tongue with joyful shouting.
Then they said among the nations, "The LORD has done great things for them."
The LORD has done great things for us. We are glad.   – Psalm 126:1-3

We have rejoiced watching You liberate families and friends from spiritual captivity. When they speak of the change You bring to them, they talk about feeling free. This freedom can seem too good to be true, like a dream. We dare to pray this dream for others: that thousands will jailbreak at once, breaking free from darkness all at the same time. As such movements of mass repentance become a reality, distant places will publicize the news. You will be honored. There will be joy in the streets, expressly thanking You for the great things You have done. And as promised, we will be glad. Weeping glad. Howling with glee glad.

But we had to celebrate and rejoice, for this brother of yours was dead
and has begun to live, and was lost and has been found.   – Luke 15:32

Even one person coming home to You is no small thing. But if thousands return home all at once, the joy will be even greater. Let the celebration begin! Draw many back to Yourself and set our city rejoicing. *Pray:*

  • for God to be glorified by new movements to Christ.
  • for Christians to experience the joy of the Father when He regains His lost daughters and sons.

In all their affliction He was afflicted...In His love and in His mercy He redeemed them, and He lifted them and carried them all the days of old.
– Isaiah 63:9

Seeking God for... **Disabled People**

Pray that they will be surrounded with loving friends and family; for steady refreshment of their hearts toward God; for physical stamina and healing; for endurance through chronic pain; for financial provision to cover the cost of therapy and special care; that they will know and display the love of God.

Prayerwalk: Pray along the same route that a person with disabilities might use to move through your neighborhood, school or workplace.

...on behalf of the **Middle East**
Egypt, Iran, Iraq

for joy as He answers prayer

You who hears prayer, to You all people will come...
By awesome deeds You answer us in righteousness,
O God of our salvation, You who are the trust of all the ends of the earth...
They who dwell in the ends of the earth stand in awe of Your signs.
You make the dawn and the sunset shout for joy. – Psalm 65:2, 5, 8

How marvelous You are for hearing prayers every day, from every place and people on earth. Because of Your mercy, You have answered some of our smallest prayers in great ways. Enlarge our praying to match Your purpose to glorify Your Son. Bring great changes to our families and our cities. Do far more than we have dared to ask, so that we praise You with grateful amazement. Make a holy spectacle of Your tender, kingly power. Cause people to stand in awe. Satisfy those who have waited patiently for Your goodness with tears of joy.

―――――――――――――――――――――

"What do you want Me to do for you?" And he said, "Lord, I want to regain my sight!" And Jesus said to him, "Receive your sight; your faith has made you well." Immediately he regained his sight and began following Him, glorifying God; and when all the people saw it, they gave praise to God. – Luke 18:41-43

You have called us to call on You. We find courage to seek You for our deepest desires. Let our prayers bring You open glory by moving many to praise You. *Pray:*

• for outbreaks of praise to God from the people in our city as they see new displays of Christ's power.

• for Christ to answer those who cry out to Him for help.

Seeking God for... **Marriages**

> *Marriage should be honored by all.*
> – Hebrews 13:4 NIV

Thank God for sturdy marriages that reflect His faithfulness and beauty. Pray especially for marriages which are strained to a breaking point or are failing, that God will bring both hope and help; that He will heal broken hearts and restore intimacy; for every marriage, that God will refresh and re-center homes in Christ.

Prayerwalk: Pray for the married couples living in your neighborhood.

...on behalf of the **Middle East**
Israel, Jordan, Kuwait

DAY 36

Wednesday
April 1

SEEKING GOD...

to restore desolate communities

You're going to look at this place, these empty and desolate...streets of Jerusalem, and say, "A wasteland. Unlivable. Not even a dog could live here."
But the time is coming when you're going to hear laughter and celebration, marriage festivities, people exclaiming, "Thank GOD of the Angel Armies. He's so good! His love never quits"...I'll make everything as good as new. – Jeremiah 33:10-11 The Message

We call upon You to visit neighborhoods that many consider to be unlivable or even God-forsaken. But Your love endures forever. You have not forsaken the people who live in desolate places. Renew many people by the power of the gospel. Redeem whole families. Set heaven's song ringing in their hearts so that joy pours out of the windows and doors. As they rejoice with praise, their laughter will be contagious and others will join the celebration of how good You really are.

When the Lord saw her, He felt compassion for her, and said to her, "Do not weep." And He came up and touched the coffin... And He said, "Young man, I say to you, arise!"...And Jesus gave him back to his mother... They began glorifying God, saying..."God has visited His people!" – Luke 7:13-16

Many walk in aching sadness, as if life were a funeral procession. They have almost buried their hope for lost loved ones. Act again in Your vast compassion. Raise them by Your power. Bring nothing less than the visitation of God. *Pray:*

- for Christ to speak with compassion and power to those locked in grief, saying to them, "Do not weep!"
- for Christ to give life to those who are lost to Him.

On the day the LORD gives you relief from suffering and turmoil and cruel bondage. – Isaiah 14:3 NIV

Seeking God for...Substance Abusers

Pray that God will break every form of bondage, including alcoholism and drug addiction. Pray for wise counselors to bring timely intervention and counsel. Pray that God will heal the substance abusers' minds and bodies. Pray that they will turn from a life of addiction to a life of serving others in Christ.

Prayerwalk: Consider those in your neighborhood who may be bound in some kind of addiction, asking God to free them in Christ.

...on behalf of the **Middle East**
Lebanon, Libya, Morocco

for abundance
with contentment

Thursday
April 2

They will come and shout for joy...and they will be radiant
over the bounty of the Lord – over the grain and the new wine and the oil...
And their life will be like a watered garden...
> *for I will turn their mourning into joy*
> *and will comfort them and give them joy for their sorrow...*
> *and My people will be satisfied with My goodness.* — Jeremiah 31:12-14

You have promised to change the hearts of Your people, so that
they will recognize the bounty of Your blessing as evidence of Your
love. Fulfill this promise in our day. Give Your people the radiant joy
of grateful contentment. Do much more than merely improve our
circumstances. Touch the sadness of our souls. Heal our warped
ambitions. Dispel our jealousies and mindless cravings for what
does not matter. Cause our economy to bloom and our hearts to
flourish in generosity so that Your blessing abounds for all.

Do not be afraid, little flock, for your Father has chosen gladly
to give you the kingdom. — Luke 12:32

Like sheep we are easily alarmed and unable to survive on our own.
Reveal how glad You really are to give us all that we need, and more:
the abundance of Your kingdom. *Pray:*

- for the hearts of people to be changed so that they turn away
  from what disappoints to experience God's goodness.

- for Christ's followers to find joy in the safety and plenitude
  of the Father's love.

Seeking God for...Ministries

**Pray that Christian ministries
will be founded on God's truth,
anointed by God's power and
well-supported by God's people.
Pray for those who labor
in specialized ministries to
effectively increase the impact
of local churches.**

**Prayerwalk: Find a high point
from which you can see much of
the community. Pray that God
would send needed Christian
workers to your city and at
the same time send Christian
workers from your city.**

*Finally, brothers,
pray for us that the
word of the Lord
will spread rapidly
and be glorified, just
as it did also with you.*
— 2 Thessalonians 3:1

...on behalf of the **Middle East**
Oman, Qatar, Saudi Arabia

Friday
April 3

for joy in extravagant worship

*And the singers sang...and on that day they offered great sacrifices,
    rejoicing because God had given them great joy.
The women and children also rejoiced.
The sound of rejoicing in Jerusalem could be heard far away.*   – Nehemiah 12:42-43 NIV

You sent a wave of joy upon Your people as they celebrated what You had done for their city. You helped them give You heartfelt praise. The truth and beauty of Your love became clearer as their songs became louder. In our day and in our city, may this kind of joy overflow in exuberant celebrations of sincere worship. May the work of Your Spirit and the word of Your truth fix our attention upon Your Son. Cause whole families and generations to be joined in the joy of honoring You. Even now You are worthy of widespread renown for Your work in our city. Give us confidence to expect even greater days of praise.

———————————————————

*As soon as He was approaching, near the descent of the Mount of Olives,
the whole crowd of the disciples began to praise God joyfully
with a loud voice for all the miracles which they had seen.*   – Luke 19:37

Ignite extravaganzas of public praise for all the things You have already done. Set our hearts ablaze with expectant joy for the greater things You will do. *Pray:*

- for zealous worship, expressing full hearts with full-volume joy.
- for miraculous works of Christ to be remembered and celebrated.
- for God to be openly praised in the public square of our culture.

Now Abraham was old, advanced in age; and the LORD had blessed Abraham in every way.
— Genesis 24:1

Seeking God for...**Elderly People**

Pray that God's strength and peace will be poured out on those who are advanced in years. Pray for them to be honored and cared for so that loneliness would be banished with lasting friendships and family bonds. Pray for grace and strength to deal with illness.

Pray that their latter years will be significant, reflecting the glory of God.

Prayerwalk: Pray for one or two elderly people you know in your neighborhood. Or pray at a retirement community or an extended care facility.

...on behalf of the **Middle East**
Syria, Tunisia, Turkey

for joy in His presence

"Sing for joy and be glad, O daughter of Zion;
for behold I am coming and I will dwell in your midst," declares the LORD.
   "Many nations will join themselves to the Lord in that day
   and will become My people. Then I will dwell in your midst."   – Zechariah 2:10-11

This is Your promise: In the day that many nations come to You,
You will come to them, manifesting Your presence in an exchange
of joy and honor. Even so, come, Lord of all the earth! Your promise
is being fulfilled. Even now we see entire peoples coming to You.
Many who have resisted Your call for centuries are now turning to
seek You. Other peoples are hearing Your voice for the first time.
Call them all, loud and clear. Draw them together with those who
have already joined themselves to You, the risen Lord of glory.
Set our hearts on fire with expectancy that You will certainly come,
as if returning home, to peoples and places all over the earth.
May our welcome song be loud, and the joy of our love be great.
Even so, come, Lord Jesus.

While they were telling these things, He Himself stood in their midst.   – Luke 24:36

Just as You, the risen Lord, entered the room filled with Your followers,
we ask You to manifest Your presence to all who love You. *Pray:*

- for Christ to reveal His living presence to those who love Him.
- for Christ to be welcomed by many who have yet to follow Him.

Seeking God for... **Prisoners** *and their* **Families**

Pray that people in prisons
will hear the gospel and
follow Christ; for fellowships
of believers to multiply; for
prisoners to be guarded from
violence and forces of spiritual
evil. Pray that the spouses and
children of prisoners would be
protected and provided for.

Pray for released prisoners to
find strength and wisdom
to live abundant lives.

Prayerwalk: Pray near a jail
or a correctional facility. Or pray
for homes in your neighborhood
that may have family members
or loved ones in prison.

You who seek God,
let your heart revive.
For the LORD hears
the needy and does
not despise His who
are prisoners.
     – Psalm 69:32-33

...on behalf of the **Middle East**

United Arab Emirates, Yemen

51

The importance of Palm Sunday

The event we have come to call "Palm Sunday" shines as a prophetic portrait of the spiritual awakening Christ desires to bring. Jesus not only initiated the procession, but He refused to shut it down. He was doing more than merely fulfilling prophecy. He was prophesying, presenting a lasting vision of how He will be recognized in the midst of hostility at the end of the age. Christ will be followed by some in every people. He will be welcomed, at least by a few, in every place. Palm Sunday gives us a vision of the global spiritual awakening we are praying toward.

Preparing the way by prayer

Jesus prepared the way for Palm Sunday by sending His followers to pray on-site in many communities (Luke 10:1-2). The prayers of these ordinary followers were publicly prayed and then openly answered. God was being honored. Because of their prayers, Jesus was becoming famous even in places where He had not visited. There was growing expectancy that God would do even greater things.

A crescendo of welcoming praise

The raising of Lazarus touched off an explosion of welcoming praise (John 12:18). The dramatic answer to Jesus' prayer for His friend Lazarus (John 11:41-43) got everyone talking about all they had seen God do in the lives of their friends and neighbors in other places. Luke says the crowd was praising God "for all the miracles which they had seen" (Luke 19:37). Grateful praise for many answered prayers quickly became a crescendo of welcoming worship.

The event we have come to call "Palm Sunday" shines as a prophetic portrait of the spiritual awakening Christ desires to bring.

Palm Sunday
The hope of Christ's visitation

A lasting movement

Thousands of people gathered at the temple with Jesus early every morning, hanging on His every word (Luke 21:38). The Palm Sunday worshipers should not be confused with the much smaller mob which shouted for Jesus' execution later in the week. That crowd was incited by Christ's enemies, who were forced to arrest Jesus by night "because they were afraid of the people" – the very throng that had welcomed and honored Him daily with increasing devotion (Luke 22:2, Mark 14:1-2).

A prophetic portrait

Palm Sunday is sometimes dismissed as if it were a political rally gone wrong. But Jesus was all for it. He planned whatever could have been planned. And He refused to silence the celebration. He said that rocks would have cried out if the people had been restrained (Luke 19:40). The intensity mounted. The crowds increased. Eventually "all the city was stirred, saying, 'Who is this?'" (Matthew 21:10). Those who hadn't yet personally encountered Jesus were eager to know more. If Jesus was giving us any indication of how God desires to visit communities with transforming power, we are right in praying for this kind of receptive glory to sweep throughout whole cities.

The hope of visitation:
His arrival more than our revival

Hated or praised, Christ was then what He will be again: the sole focus of attention of whole cities in days of great spiritual awakening. Our best prayers are prayers of welcome – that the risen Jesus Himself will be recognized and received throughout entire communities. Whenever there has been revival, it has been a partial fulfillment of the promise of Palm Sunday. Now, more than ever, it's time to invite Christ the Lord to bring His life-giving presence upon our cities.

> *Whenever there has been revival, it has been a partial fulfillment of the promise of Palm Sunday.*

On Palm Sunday, Jesus was rejected by a few, which caused Him to weep. But He was also welcomed by many.

Day after day people thronged to Him and His teaching, celebrating the wonders of the coming kingdom. Palm Sunday may be the clearest picture we have of how God visits an entire community with His transforming power. Today we celebrate the hope that God will visit His people throughout the world to glorify Himself before the end of the age.

Blessed is the One who comes in the name of the Lord.
– Psalm 118:26

The earth is the LORD'S, and all it contains,
the world, and those who dwell in it...
Lift up your heads, O gates,
and be lifted up, O ancient doors,
    that the King of glory may come in!
      Who is the King of glory?
      The LORD strong and mighty,
      the LORD mighty in battle!
Lift up your heads, O gates,
and lift them up, O ancient doors,
    that the King of glory may come in!
      Who is this King of glory?
      The LORD of hosts. He is the King of glory!
– Psalm 24:1, 7-10

to fill the world with His glory

Who is this King of glory? The LORD of hosts! He is the King of glory! – Psalm 24:10

Visit Your people in ways that will rock the nations and turn the attention of all upon You. Come! Find our city prepared by our prayers to welcome You. Manifest Your presence, even though our eyes may not yet behold You physically. Reveal the great majesty of Your wisdom. Show the surpassing grandeur of Your governing love. Display the dreadful magnificence of Your wrath against evil. Reveal Your fierce passion for Your beloved bride.

Many who do not know You will sense that You are near. They will ask, "Who is this?" And we will know who You are. We have sought You in the night. We have wrestled like Jacob to lay hold of Your promise. We have sought Your face. Yes, we will know who You are. We will name You with welcoming passion: "You are the King of glory!" Even so, Lord Jesus, come!

The crowds...were shouting, "Hosanna to the Son of David! Blessed is He who comes in the name of the LORD. Hosanna in the highest!" When He had entered Jerusalem, all the city was stirred, saying, "Who is this?"
– Matthew 21:9-10

When You come upon our city, reveal Your presence so clearly that many are filled with wonder to know who You are. *Pray:*

- for Christ to capture the attention and desire of many who have ignored or rejected Him.

- for believers to be filled with expectant love for Christ.

Seeking God for...**the Coming Generation**

Pray that many who are now children will soon become passionate followers of Christ; that during their lifetimes they will finish evangelizing the world; that they will endure suffering to overcome evil and bring forth the promised blessing of God upon all peoples; that they will give Christ the finest whole-life worship of all history.

Prayerwalk: Walk your city thinking of people who will live there in years to come. Pray for the generation that will be dwelling in your city when Christ returns.

How often I wanted to gather your children together, the way a hen gathers her chicks under her wings, and you were unwilling... From now on you will not see Me until you say, "Blessed is He who comes in the name of the Lord!"
– Matthew 23:37, 39

...on behalf of **Jerusalem**
Pray for God's peace and glory to be upon Jerusalem.

On **PRAYER MISSION** with Christ

"For the Son of Man has come to seek and to save that which was lost." – Luke 19:10

God is calling us to join Him in what we could call "prayer mission," praying beyond the boundaries of our homes and churches in order to pray our way into the lives of people.

Prayer is more than a technique to obtain God's blessing for your own life. Prayer is God's way of inviting you to join Him as He works in other people's lives.

We **seek** those who are lost by prayer,

and we **serve** them by Christ's kindness,

so that Christ will **save** many by the power of the gospel.

To **SEEK, SERVE** and **SAVE**

As we do the seeking, Christ will do the saving.

Jesus said that His mission was "to seek and to save" people who were lost to God (Luke 19:10). The risen Christ pursues that same mission today. He gives every believer a way to join with Him in *seeking* people by prayer, *serving* them by demonstrating His kindness, and introducing them to Himself so that they too, will experience His *saving* love.

Prayer leads to *Care*, opening ways to *Share*

Persistent, life-giving *Prayer* for others
leads to opportunities to *Care*, displaying God's love,
which opens the way to *Share* the gospel, declaring God's love.

Another way to describe a **prayer-care-share**
lifestyle is to **seek** and to **serve**, in order to **save**.

SEEK
with focused prayer

"I am among you as one who serves." – Luke 22:27

Beyond known needs: Pray your way into their story.

We often form our prayers around needs we see or requests we hear. But people don't always know what they really need. That's why their prayer requests often fall short of the big picture of what God desires to do in their lives.

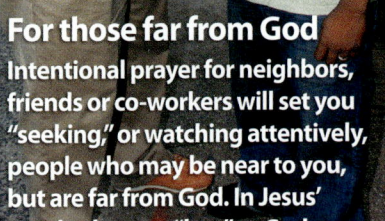

For those far from God
Intentional prayer for neighbors, friends or co-workers will set you "seeking," or watching attentively, people who may be near to you, but are far from God. In Jesus' words, they are "lost" to God.

Pray with scripture to pray in hope.

As you learn to pray with scripture, you will be praying your way into the great story that God is unfolding in families, businesses, neighborhoods, peoples and cities.

SERVE
with acts of kindness

As we do the seeking, we will find God's way of serving.

As you envision God's best intentions for particular people with your prayers, you will be considering their story and their future. You will be seeking them along with God.

People may have no idea that anyone is praying for them. But as you pray, look for God to open practical ways for you to serve the very people you have been praying for with simple acts of kindness.

Kindness:
God's love on display

Discover the joy of demonstrating God's love in practical, tangible ways. To those you already know, creative kindness can be as simple as offering co-workers a cup of coffee, or giving a neighbor a few freshly-baked cookies.

Don't be afraid to show kindness to those you don't know. Team up with others (bring a friend, or your kids!) to give out bottles of cold water on a hot day, or offer a simple service like washing windows in your neighborhood.

Great resources for many more good ideas

Steve Sjogren has developed some good resources designed to help ordinary people show God's love in practical ways. He has hundreds of tested ideas. Go to **www.KindnessResources.com**.

SAVE —
by helping people follow Christ

"They will declare the work of God, and will consider what He has done." – Psalm 64:9

Simplicity and sincerity: Following God's lead

Instead of dreading evangelism as something that will make you a bother or a bore, you will find yourself following God's lead with timely authenticity and heartfelt sincerity.

Co-working with God

As you pray and display God's kindness in practical ways, watch for God-given opportunities to share His love. They can come up suddenly with such perfect timing that it's hard not to believe that you are co-working with God.

Confidence to be His story-teller

Because you've been praying along with God's word and heart, don't be surprised to find that ideas to creatively convey God's love occur to you.

As you pray God's story, you will find confidence to tell your own story to communicate the gospel in fresh, relevant ways.

People and **Places**
I'm praying for

People I'm praying for:

Focus your praying for a few particular people throughout the 40 days.

1. Ask the Holy Spirit to impress you with the names of people who are far from Christ but near to you. Write their names below.

2. Use the ideas and truths of the daily scripture selections to pray in creative ways for these people.

3. Watch how God may open ways for you to show His kindness and to share the gospel with them.

_____

_____

_____

Places I'm prayerwalking:

Pray on-site in places where you live, work or play. Sometimes getting closer helps you pray clearer. Praying in the places where you expect God to answer your prayers will help you envision the fulfillment of His promises – building your faith, lifting your hope and increasing your love.

Each of the 40 days includes a practical idea for prayerwalking. Aim to prayerwalk at least three times. Record some of the places where you prayerwalk below.

Near my home: _____

Near my workplace: _____

Near a place new to me: _____

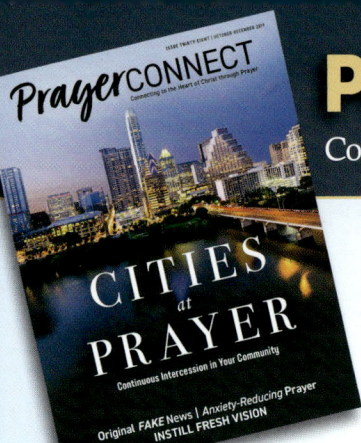

PRAYERCONNECT

Connecting to the heart of Christ through prayer

Equip prayer leaders
> with tools to disciple their congregations.

Mobilize believers
> to pray for their church, city and the nations.

Connect intercessors
> with the growing prayer movement.

A quarterly magazine. Each issue includes:

- Practical articles equip and inspire your prayer life.
- Helpful prayer tips and proven ideas.
- News of prayer movements around the world.
- Theme articles exploring important prayer topics.

Three different ways to subscribe

(four issues a year):

$24.99 - **Print** *(includes digital version)*
$19.99 - **Digital**
$35.99 - **Membership**
> in Church Prayer Leaders Network
> *(includes print, digital and CPLN benefit)*

Subscribe now.

Order at **www.prayerconnect.net** or call 800-217-5200.

30 Days of Prayer *for the Muslim World*
April 24 – May 23, 2020

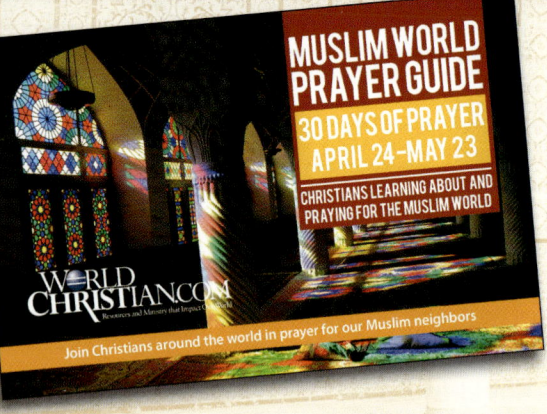

Join millions of Christians around the world who pray for Muslims during the very days that Muslims are praying. These 30 days coincide with the prayer season of Ramadan. It is an ideal time for Christians worldwide to make an intentional effort to learn about, pray for and reach out to Muslim neighbors – across the street and around the world.

The full-color prayer guide is available in two versions: adults and kids.

Published by:

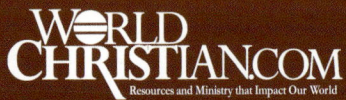

Find out more from **30DaysPrayer.com**.
Bulk prices when you order as few as 10 copies.

Order from WayMakers online or by phone:
WayMakers.org · 800-264-5214

You can also order from **WorldChristian.com**.

"That every tongue confess that Jesus Christ is Lord."

– Philippians 2:11

MARCH FOR JESUS

MAY 30, 2020

Celebrating one thing
upon which we all agree:

Jesus Christ
is Lord!

The *March For Jesus* is a procession
of praise through the streets of the city
to celebrate the Lordship of Jesus Christ.
Worshipping openly together exalts and declares
the honor, majesty and glory of Jesus.

Register your city!
Help organize a march!

To register, learn more,
or find the nearest march go to:
www.TheMarchForJesus.org

Write to:
info@TheMarchForJesus.org

WayMakers Resources

ITEM	DISCOUNT	COST *	QUANTITY	TOTAL
SEEK GOD FOR THE CITY 2020				
or CLAMA A DIOS POR LA CIUDAD 2020**				
1-19 copies		$ 3.00 each		
20-99 copies	20%	$ 2.40 each		
100-249 copies	35%	$ 1.95 each		
250-499 copies	55%	$ 1.35 each		
PROMPTS FOR PRAYERWALKERS		$ 2.00 each		
LIGHT FROM MY HOUSE		$ 2.00 each		
OPEN MY CITY		$ 2.00 each		
WHAT WOULD JESUS PRAY?		$ 2.00 each		
BLESSINGS		$ 2.00 each		
THE LORD IS THEIR SHEPHERD		$ 2.00 each		
PRAYERWALKING	25%	$ 9.00 each		

	Subtotal	
	Texas residents add 8.25% sales tax	
	Shipping and Handling (Minimum $5)	
	Donation to WayMakers (Optional)	
	TOTAL	

SHIPPING & HANDLING

$ 1 – $ 10	$ 5.00
$ 11 – $ 30	$ 7.00
$ 31 – $ 75	20% of order
$ 76 and up	13% of order

PLEASE SHIP TO: (Please provide a street address. UPS cannot deliver to a Post Office Box.)

Name

Organization

Street Address

City   State   ZIP

Phone   E-mail

VISA / MC / Disc / AmEx   Expires

Name on card

* Please call to learn about quantity discounts (up to 60%) on most items!

** **Seek God for the City** in Spanish is available at the same prices. Order online, or call us to combine English and Spanish in the same order. **Clama a Dios por la Ciudad** está disponible al mismo precio que en inglés. Llámenos para combinar libros en inglés y español en la misma orden.

Please order early to allow normal delivery time of two weeks (but many orders can be fulfilled last minute!). Order **Seek God for the City** before February 10 to be sure of getting all the copies you need. Supplies are limited. Additional shipping costs may be required after February 17. Please include payment with your order. Please calculate and include payment for shipping costs. Thanks! For quickest delivery, call us. Make checks payable to WayMakers. Please send this form with payment to:

WayMakers
PO Box 203131
Austin, TX 78720-3131

Phone   (512) 419-7729
           (800) 264-5214
Web   www.waymakers.org